AMERICAN BATTLESHIPS

....

A Pictorial History

FLEET LEAVING BREST

U.S. Battleship fleet, Division 9, Leaving Brest, France, on Dec. 16, 1918, following the end of World War I on Nov. 11. Ships in the fleet included: *Pennsylvania* (BB-38), *Oklahoma* (BB-37), *Nevada* (BB-36), *New York* (BB-34), *Texas* (BB-35), *Arkansas* (BB-33), *Wyoming* (BB-32), *Florida* (BB-30), and *Delaware* (BB-28). The newer ships are in the lead.

AMERICAN BATTLESHIPS

*A pictorial history of BB-1 to BB-71,
with prototypes Maine & Texas*

....

By Max R. Newhart

PICTORIAL HISTORIES PUBLISHING CO
Missoula, Montana

Library of Congress Catalog Card Number 95-78913

ISBN 1-57510-004-5

First Printing: August 1995
Revised Printing: May 1996

Publishing Coordinator: Stan Cohen.

Pictorial Histories Publishing Co., Inc.
713 South Third West
Missoula, Montana 59801

CONTENTS

ACKNOWLEDGEMENTS

I WOULD LIKE TO THANK each of the following individuals for their constructive comments during the period of my writing this book. Each in their own way being cognizant of their input or not were a great deal of help.

Stan Cohen for his early conversations and final commitment to publish the book. His overview and decision to publish an unknown author of a very special topic of great interest and pride to many individuals.

Captain Ben Blee, USN (Ret.) for his comments when he granted literary permission for excerpts from his book, *Battleship, North Carolina (BB-55)*. I tried to follow them with due respect.

Tom Taplin for his comments, first proofreading of the book and his encouragement to complete the book.

The personnel and the National Archives & Records Administration, Cardiographic Branch, and particularly, Mr. Chuck Haberlien and Mr. Ed. Finney of the Naval Historical Foundation Photo Service at the Washington Navy Yard for their assistance in obtaining many of the photos you see in this book.

Elizabeth, my wife, for her total backing and support in my endeavor. She would proofread for proper English, then listen to my haggling to her comments. She also helped guide me to obtain a publisher and work the book to its completion. A terrific woman a man would always like to have at his side.

PREFACE

AS AN ENTHUSIAST OF HISTORY since childhood, I, as have many, have found different topics which have stimulated additional interest as more is learned about a certain subject.

The battleship, and later more specific, the American battleship became that certain subject several years ago. First in just general reading, then deeper into the history of the ships as I learned the variations which were studied and developed during the course of the battleships' evolution.

During the research for information, I found many well written books on the battleship. Some on a single ship (the ship's data books), a class of ships, a series of the classes of ships, several on most of the ships, one on the design history of all, and finally, the *Dictionary of American Naval Fighting Ships*, an eight volume set of information listing every American fighting ship since the beginning of the U.S. Navy.

After reading many and searching through many more, I felt there might be a desire for a book for the enthusiast, condensed in history, construction and technical information and material, but complete in that every American battleship would have its own data outline and photograph, and list its own personal information from the date of congressional authorization to its final disposition.

The technical data listed primarily as the ships were originally commissioned, but with notes in (bracketed information on the Individual Data Sheets), to show some of their upgrades and refits. These upgrades and refits completed on the ships in active service just prior to, during and after World War II. Also on the Iowa class in their general configuration completed during their latest recommissionings during the 1980s.

The Construction and Operational Histories note only the major items and history points for the battleships during their careers. The many other books available note the in-depth profiles on each ship, which is beyond the scope of this book.

With this book, perhaps a student of history, a naval enthusiast, or an up and coming "future old salt," may use it as the stepping stone to seek out all that has been written about the battleship or as the book to be used for general reference knowledge.

Use its contents for your intended or obtained results and enjoy the marvelous history that these ships have to offer, as you go from the prototype *USS Maine* (BB-00/ ACR-1), through to the uncompleted *USS Louisiana* (BB-71) of the cancelled Montana class.

CONSTRUCTION HISTORY

THE MODERN BATTLESHIP can trace its ancestry back to the ironclads with their steam drives, turreted guns, and armored hulls. Those humble beginnings are with the Union's *USS Monitor* and the Confederate's *CSS Virginia (Merrimac)* of the American Civil War and their historic engagement of March 9, 1862 at Hampton Roads.[1]

If we consider these two ships as our beginning then the ironclads that followed, based on John Ericsson's design (low-freeboard turreted gunship), will fill the period from 1862 to 1901 and include such names as the *USS Miantonomoh, USS Monadnock, USS Amphitrite, USS Tonopah, USS Cheyenne, USS Wampanoag* and *USS Puritan.*

William B. Hunt, Secretary of the Navy from 1881 to 1882, and his successor William E. Chandler initiated and continued work which came to be known as the "New Navy." Their work resulted in Congress authorizing three steel cruisers (*Atlanta, Boston* and *Chicago*) and a dispatch boat (*Dolphin*) in 1883. These ships, the famous "ABCDs," constituted the first ships of the "New Navy."[2]

Chandler's successor, William C. Whitney, who served from 1885 to 1889, brings us to our "battleship," with the Congressional authorization of two heavy-armored cruisers (later to be re-classified second-class battleships) *USS Maine* (BB-00/ACR-1) at 6,682 tons standard displacement, a speed of 17 knots with largest armament of 4-10"/35 guns and *USS Texas* (BB-000) at 6,315 tons standard displacement, a speed of 17 knots with largest armament of 2-12"/35 guns, and the higher freeboard which the monitors lacked.[3]

(Note: The designations of BB-00 and BB-000 for the *USS Maine* and *USS Texas* are arbitrary numbers assigned by the author during research in order to maintain differentiation from the later ships when the "BB" was formally adopted on July 17, 1920 as the Navy completed its assignments of ships' hull numbers and back numbered them to the earlier ships.)

USS Maine laid down on October 17, 1888, with commissioning on September 17, 1895, and *USS Texas* laid down June 1, 1889 with commissioning on August 15, 1895, were actually the prototypes for the battleships which followed. Each of the prototypes being slightly different in order to try various new naval engineering concepts of the time in their designs.

American battleships can then be divided into groups for their history: the Prototypes, Pre-Dreadnoughts, Post-Dreadnoughts, and finally the Fast Battleships. Each group is then sub-divided into the subsequent classes which are the single or more ships of the same general design that came about during the evolutionary steps. As technology developed and battle lessons learned they were incorporated into the design, construction, and armaments.

The Prototypes, only two, are as listed previously. The Pre-Dreadnoughts were the next (25) ships, beginning with *USS Indiana* (BB-01), keel laid on May 7, 1891 and commissioned November 20, 1895 at 10,288 tons standard displacement and a largest armament of 4-13"/35 guns and ending with *USS New Hampshire* (BB-25), keel laid on May 1, 1905 and commissioned March 19, 1908 at 16,000 tons standard displacement and a largest armament of 4-12"/45guns.

The Pre-Dreadnoughts are described as such because they were built with mixed caliber main armament.

The main reason for the Pre-Dreadnought designation is that these ships of the American Navy and all other world Navies were built before the British warship of the Royal Navy, *HMS Dreadnought* 17,900 tons standard displacement with main armament of 10-12"/45 guns, was commissioned in 1909 as the first battleship with the main armament of the single caliber design, and the main armament along the center line of the ship. This arrangement was considered superior and believed to render all previous battleships obsolete.

(It should be noted that the Americans were aware of this advantage and had actually laid the keel during the same time for *USS South Carolina* (BB-26), but *HMS Dreadnought* was commissioned first and therefore became the first ship of the type.)

The Post-Dreadnoughts numbered a total of 29 ships beginning with *USS South Carolina* (BB-26), keel laid on December 18, 1906 and commissioned March 1, 1910 at 16,000 tons standard displacement with a main armament of 8-12"/45 guns and ending with *USS Massachusetts* (BB-54), keel laid on April 4, 1921, but cancelled before completion by the signing of the Washington Naval Conference Treaty on February 8, 1922 at 43,200 tons standard displacement with a projected design main armament of 12-16"/50 guns. Of these 29 ships, 7 were never completed as a result of American compliance to its signing the agreement of the stipulations to the Washington Naval Conference Treaty. Construction on the 7 ships was suspended with their dispositions noted in the individual ships profiles.

During the period of 1916–1917 other battleship designs were also studied, resulting in ship designs of up to 80,000 tons standard displacement and main battery armaments of up to 12-18"/48 caliber. These design studies were completed at the request of Senator Benjamin R. Tillman of South Carolina. Senator Tillman, as the chairman of the Senate Naval Affairs Committee, requested the studies in order to determine "the ultimate limits of battleship growth." The results of the investigation showed "the Panama Canal was the main limit on the ships length at 975 feet and beam 108 feet; and harbor depths limited their draft to 34 feet (about 32'9" in normal condition)." Designs considered in developing these conclusions were 70,000, 80,000, and 63,000 ton standard displacements. None of these designs were ever requested by the Department of the Navy for construction or submitted for Congressional approval.[4]

Fast battleships included a total of 12 ships beginning with *USS North Carolina* (BB-55), keel laid on October 27, 1937 and commissioned April 9, 1941 at 36,600 tons standard displacement with a main armament of 9-16"/45 guns and ending with *USS Kentucky* (BB-66), keel laid on December 6, 1944 and construction permanently suspended on February 17, 1947 at 45,000 tons standard displacement with a main armament of 9-16"/50 guns.

A final battleship was to be built as the ultimate in battleship development, but was not to be as fast as the fast battleships, and included a projected five (5) ships beginning with *USS Montana* (BB-67) and ending with *USS Louisiana* (BB-71) and originally to have been constructed from 1941 to 1947 at 60,500 tons standard displacement with a main armament of 12-16"/50 guns.

Battleships were named after the States, continuing the tradition that was established by the Navy in 1817 of reserving the State titles for "battleships/ships of the line."

During the period of construction history of the battleships, at least one ship was named for each state of the union, some states were named several times, except for Alaska and Hawaii which were not yet in the statehood. When a new battleship was named for a current ship, the older ship was either reclassified, renamed or decommissioned and scrapped.

Note: On the following table, the ships identified with an (*) were upgraded and modified using the equipment and machinery from the ships cancelled and scrapped in compliance with the provisions covered by the signing of the Washington Naval Treaty of February 8, 1922 and the London Naval Treaty of April 22, 1930.

The ships identified with an (**) were upgraded and improved during refits and repairs following battle damage during World War II. All active ships were upgraded for improved anti-aircraft defense during World War II.

During World War II the ten fast battleships with their upgraded and improved anti-aircraft weapons were able to provide the air defense ring around the fleet carriers because their speed capabilities were able to match the carriers speeds.

The ships identified (***), the Iowa Class, were of course upgraded during the 1980s as each was recommissioned for what may have been their last time. Two of them served with distinction during Operation Desert Shield and Operation Desert Storm, *Missouri* (BB-63) and *Wisconsin* (BB-64).

. . . .

USS *Maine* (BB-00/ACR-1)
USS *Texas* (BB-000)
USS *Indiana* (BB-01)
USS *Massachusetts* (BB-02)
USS *Oregon* (BB-03)
USS *Iowa* (BB-04)
USS *Kearsarge* (BB-05)
USS *Kentucky* (BB-06)
USS *Illinois* (BB-07)
USS *Alabama* (BB-08)
USS *Wisconsin* (BB-09)
USS *Maine* (BB-10)
USS *Missouri* (BB-11)
USS *Ohio* (BB-12)
USS *Virginia* (BB-13)
USS *Nebraska* (BB-14)
USS *Georgia* (BB-15)
USS *New Jersey* (BB-16)
USS *Rhode Island* (BB-17)

USS *Connecticut* (BB-18)
USS *Louisiana* (BB-19)
USS *Vermont* (BB-20)
USS *Kansas* (BB-21)
USS *Minnesota* (BB-22)
USS *Mississippi* (BB-23)
USS *Idaho* (BB-24)
USS *New Hampshire* (BB-25)
USS *South Carolina* (BB-26)
USS *Michigan* (BB-27)
USS *Delaware* (BB-28)
USS *North Dakota* (BB-29)
USS *Florida* (BB-30)
USS *Utah* (BB-31/AG-16)
USS *Wyoming* (BB-32/AG-17)
USS *Arkansas* (*) (BB-33)
USS *New York* (**) (BB-34)
USS *Texas* (*) (**)(BB-35)
USS *Nevada* (*)(**) (BB-36)

USS *Oklahoma* (*) (BB-37)
USS *Pennsylvania* (*)(**) (BB-38)
USS *Arizona* (*) (BB-39)
USS *New Mexico* (*)(**) (BB-40)
USS *Mississippi* (*) (**)(BB-41/ AG-128)
USS *Idaho* (*)(**) (BB-42)
USS *Tennessee* (**) (BB-43)
USS *California* (**) (BB-44)
USS *Colorado* (**) (BB-45)
USS *Maryland* (**) (BB-46)
USS *Washington* (BB-47)
USS *West Virginia* (**) (BB-48)
USS *South Dakota* (BB-49)
USS *Indiana* (BB-50)
USS *Montana* (BB-51)
USS *North Carolina* (BB-52)
USS *Iowa* (BB-53)
USS *Massachusetts* (BB-54)

USS *North Carolina* (**) (BB-55)
USS *Washington* (**) (BB-56)
USS *South Dakota* (**) (BB-57)
USS *Indiana* (**) (BB-58)
USS *Massachusetts* (**) (BB-59)
USS *Alabama* (**) (BB-60)
USS *Iowa* (**)(***) (BB-61)
USS *New Jersey* (**)(***)(BB-62)
USS *Missouri* (**)(***) (BB-63)
USS *Wisconsin* (**)(***) (BB-64)
USS *Illinois* (BB-65)
USS *Kentucky* (BB-66/SCB-19)
USS *Montana* (BB-67)
USS *Ohio* (BB-68)
USS *Maine* (BB-69)
USS *New Hampshire* (BB-70)
USS *Louisiana* (BB-71)

. . . . . .

OPERATIONAL HISTORY

·················

T HE OPERATIONAL HISTORY of the American battleship as we think of it begins with the commissioning of *Texas* (BB-000) on August 15, 1895. This ship, along with the other heavy armored cruiser, both later classified as battleships, *Maine* (BB-00/ACR-1), and the four first class battleships *Indiana* (BB-01), *Massachusetts* (BB-02), *Oregon* (BB-03), and *Iowa* (BB-04) were the battleship force of the U.S. Navy when *Maine* was destroyed in Havana Harbor on the night of February 15, 1898, at 2140 hours (9:40 PM).

"Remember the *Maine*" became the battle cry as America entered into the Spanish American War on April 25, 1898.

Two significant events relating to the battleship occurred during this period. First was the sailing of the *Oregon* (BB-03) from the west coast of the United States at San Francisco, California to the east coast at Florida at Jupiter Inlet by the way of Cape Horn then on to Cuban waters in a period of 67 days (March 12, 1898, to May 24, 1898), a total of 14,700 miles. A major feat in those days, remembering the Panama Canal was not completed until 1914. Second was the first naval engagement of American battleships with a foreign fleet in the Battle of Santiago, Cuba on July 3, 1898. This battle involved *Texas* (BB-000), *Indiana* (BB-01), *Oregon* (BB-03), and *Iowa* (BB-04). *Massachusetts* (BB-02) missed the battle. She was at Guantanamo, Cuba for replenishment of her coal bunkers.[5]

Peace protocol was established between Spain and the United States on August 12, 1898, with the formal Treaty of Paris signed in November 1898 and formal approval by the United States Senate in February 1899.[6]

1900

During the year 1900 the United States had six (6) battleships in commission. Three (3) in the Pacific fleet and three (3) in the Atlantic fleet.

Each fleet operated performing normal fleet maneuvers, coastal port calls, show the flag with foreign port calls, and protecting American interests in such places as deemed necessary by the foreign policy and world politics of the time.

President Theodore Roosevelt's "Great White Fleet," sailed from Hampton Roads, Virginia on December 16, 1907, on its around-the-world cruise, covering a total of 46,000 miles and returning to Hampton Roads on February 22, 1909.

The fleet included 17 battleships, *Kearsarge* (BB-05), *Kentucky* (BB-06), *Illinois* (BB-07), *Alabama* (BB-08) (replaced by *Nebraska* in San Francisco), *Wisconsin* (BB-09), *Maine* (BB-10) (joining in San Francisco), *Missouri* (BB-11), *Ohio* (BB-12), *Virginia* (BB-13), *Nebraska* (BB-14) (joined in San Francisco relieving *Alabama*), *Georgia* (BB-15), *New Jersey* (BB-16) (Flag Ship) (commanded by R. Adm. Robley D. Evans and R. Adm. Charles S. Sperry), *Rhode Island* (BB-17), *Connecticut* (BB-18), *Louisiana* (BB-19), *Vermont* (BB-20), *Kansas* (BB-21), *Minnesota* (BB-22). Their mission purpose was to show the world American naval power and visit ports in South America, western United States, Hawaii, New Zealand, Australia, the Philippines, Japan, Egypt, Italy, and Europe.

Following the "Great White Fleet's" return, the battleships returned to their normal fleet maneuvers, overhauls, and port calls.

1910

During the year 1910, the United States Navy had a total of 30 battleships. Seventeen were on active status and 13 were in the reserve fleet or waiting decommission status. Of the 17 active ships, 16 were in the Atlantic fleet and one (1) was in the Pacific fleet. The Panama Canal was under construction, beginning 1901 with completion in 1914. 1910 the fleet continued with normal fleet drills and maneuvers with the special event of March 1, 1910, commissioning of *South Carolina* (BB-26), the first American single caliber battleship, the American "Dreadnought."

Texas (BB-000) was sunk as a target ship in Langin Sound, Chesapeake Bay 1911. Also the refloated hulk of *Maine* (BB-00) was removed from Havana Harbor and sunk with honors in the Gulf of Mexico March 16, 1912. May 28-31, 1913, in New York City at the New York Naval Station in the Commissioned Officers' mess, a memorial was dedicated to the *Maine*, commemorating her loss in Havana Harbor on February 15, 1898.

March 1914 saw several ships of the Atlantic fleet off Vera Cruz, Mexico during civil disturbances to protect American interests.

July 1914, *Mississippi* (BB-23) and *Idaho* (BB-24) both had been sold and were transferred to the Greek Navy as *Lemnos* and *Kilkis*, respectively.

Battleship design studies were under consideration for future ships which were to have tonnages up to 80,000 tons with 24-16" guns in 4 turrets of 6 guns each.[7]

April 6, 1917, U.S. entered World War I, and on December 7, 1917, the Atlantic Fleet Battleship Division 9, comprising *Delaware* (BB-28), *Florida* (BB-30), *Arkansas* (BB-33) and *New York* (BB-34), sailed to join the British Grand Fleet at Scapa Flow, as the 6th Battle Squadron, arriving on December 17. *Texas* (BB-35) arrived on February 11, 1918, upon completion of repairs following a grounding off Block Island, New York on September 27, 1917.[8]

They served with the English fleet doing convoy duty

and in blockading the German High Seas Fleet. February 6, 1918, *Wyoming* (BB-32) maneuvered to dodge a torpedo fired from a German submarine off Stavanger, Norway, one of only a few endangering engagements for American battleships during the war, as the United States Battlefleet saw only a very limited role in the war.

"Operation with the British Grand Fleet constituted the only American wartime operational experience between the Spanish-American War of 1898 and December 7, 1941, and the only wartime operational experience with large modern battle fleets".[8]

During the war, "The American Pre-Dreadnought battleships, the battleships before South Carolina (BB-26), were employed in training and in ocean convoy escort duties"[8]

November 11, 1918, ended World War I, and the fleets returned to their normal peace time fleet operations.

On August 9, 1919, the battleship anchorage for the Pacific Fleet was established at San Pedro-Long Beach, California, while the battleship anchorage for the Atlantic Fleet remained at Hampton Roads.[9]

1920

1920, and the United States Navy now had twenty (20) battleships in the active fleets, thirteen (13) in the Atlantic and seven (7) in the Pacific fleet. Also sixteen (16) in the reserve fleet consisting of the old outdated Pre-Dreadnoughts.

Both fleets continued with normal maneuvers and fleet problems.

July 17, 1920, the "BB" alpha-numeric designation for the battleship was adopted by the Navy and identified to the American battleships. All hull numbers were marked and backnumbered to the earlier ships.

November 1, 1920, *Indiana* (BB-01) was sunk while being used as a target in an important series of tests designed to determine the effectiveness of aerial bombs. She had been commissioned on November 20, 1895, and decommissioned January 31, 1919.

Construction of the six *South Dakota* class battleship (BB-49 to BB-54) keels which were laid during 1920 and 1921 was cancelled and the uncompleted hulls were scrapped during 1923 and 1924.

This resulted from the Washington Naval Conference conducted from November 11, 1921, through its completion and signing on February 8, 1922.

Also, on November 25, 1924, the incomplete *Washington* (BB-47) on which construction was suspended on February 8, 1922, of the *Colorado* class was used as a gunnery target ship and sunk. Gaining valuable data on the construction survivability yet being disposed in compliance with the Washington Naval Treaty.

Alabama (BB-08) was used as a target ship for bomb tests on September 27, 1921, and *Iowa* (BB-04) was sunk as a gunnery target ship by *Mississippi* (BB-41) in Panama Bay on March 23, 1923.

During 1922 to 1925 upgrading and modernization was considered and authorized by Congress for the battleship fleet, which required extended life following the scrapping and shipbuilding moratorium brought on by the signing of the Washington Naval Treaty. Modernizations were still being completed up to December 7, 1941. *Virginia* (BB-13) and *New Jersey* (BB-16) were sunk by bomb tests conducted by General Billy Mitchell, along with the World War I prize German battleship *Ostfriesland* on September 5, 1923.

April 24, 1924 *South Carolina* (BB-26), the first single caliber U.S. battleship, after being commissioned on March 1, 1910 and decommissioned November 10, 1923, was scrapped in compliance with the Washington Naval Treaty of 1922.

The Geneva Naval Conference was conducted from June 30 through August 27, 1927, with much discussion on naval armaments, but no agreements were reached.[10]

1930

1930, and battleship strength was at eighteen ships (18), ten (10) in the Atlantic fleet and eight (8) in the Pacific fleet. The reserve fleets were being decimated by old age and scrappage, while other newer ships were being scrapped or construction cancelled in order to be in compliance with the signing of the Washington Naval Treaty.

April 22, 1930, also concluded the London Naval Treaty, which provided yet additional constraints on the naval fleets. It added the cruiser forces with the 6 inch and 8 inch gun limitations and the continuation of the capital ship building holiday to 1936.[10]

The 1930s also saw the continued modernization of the remaining U.S. battleship fleet, with additions of the torpedo blisters to increase the ship's survivability in the event of torpedo attack, and the tripod mast replacing the cage mast. Improvements in the bridge quarters and improvements/additions of radar and gun fire controls for improved main and secondary batteries fire control.

Designs for new ships were still being studied and considered. Improvements in the ship's main battery were also underway. The last new battleship *West Virginia* (BB-48) was commissioned December 1, 1923, and only the last three (3), *Colorado* (BB-45), *Maryland* (BB-46), and *West Virginia* (BB-48), had the 16"/45 caliber guns. All preceding ships had the 14-inch main battery except for *Arkansas* (BB-33) and *Wyoming* (BB-32), which both had the 12"/50 main batteries rendering them almost unsuitable for the battleship fleet.

During 1932 through 1934, the League of Nations also conducted a Naval Disarmament Conference, but due to the weakness of the League of Nations no positive results were accomplished and no agreements were reached.[10]

December 9, 1935, concluded the Second London Naval Conference. With world political conditions at the time providing Japanese aggression in the Pacific, and Europe in the troughs of Nazism in Germany and Fascism in Italy, no additional treaty items came forth. Also, Japan had withdrawn from the conditions of the earlier naval treaties, and the nations began to rebuild their fleets. Some as history has shown for aggression, and others for their survival in the war yet to come.[10]

The oldest operational battleship in the U. S. Fleet by October 17, 1937, when the keel of *North Carolina* (BB-55) was laid, was *Arkansas* (BB-33) which was commissioned on September 17, 1912, with 12"/50 caliber guns. Both *Utah* (BB-31/AG-16) and *Wyoming* (BB-32/AG-17) having been decommissioned as battleships and converted to training ships in compliance with the Washington Naval Treaty of 1922 and the London Naval Treaty of 1930, respectively.

On May 17, 1938, congress passed the Vinson-Trammel Act authorizing the "Two-Ocean Navy," increasing U.S. naval strength, in preparation for the not too distant World War II.[11]

1940

1940, the battleship force was at seventeen (17) ships, with five (5) in the Atlantic fleet and twelve (12) in the Pacific fleet. This fleet ratio was in response to the growing tensions between the United States and Japan due to Japan's aggression in China and other areas of the far east.

April 1, 1940, the Pacific Fleet sailed to Hawaiian waters for annual fleet maneuvers, and on their conclusion were ordered to stay at Pearl Harbor as their station to act as a deterrent to hostile Japanese actions in the Pacific area.[12]

When *North Carolina* (BB-55) was commissioned April 9, 1941, she was the first of the American "Fast Battleships" and the first battleship commissioned since *West Virginia* (BB-48), December 1, 1923. Their equivalent standard displacement tonnages were at 36,600 and 37,600, respectively, but their maximum full speed was 27 knots and 21 knots, respectively. *North Carolina* having the six (6) knot speed advantage would prove a great help to the Navy during World War II. *Washington* (BB-56) was commissioned on May 15, 1941, actually giving the United States two up-to-date modern battleships before entry into the war on December 7, 1941, and ten more under construction, or authorized.

Late Sunday afternoon December 7, 1941, would place the Atlantic and Pacific Fleets in the following status with nineteen (19) ships.[13]

Pacific Fleet

Arizona (BB-39): Sunk-destroyed, never raised.
Nevada (BB-36): Damaged—returned to service May 18,1942.
Pennsylvania (BB-38): Drydock at Pearl—returned to service March 30, 1942.
Tennessee (BB-43): Damaged-returned to service Feb.25,1942.
Oklahoma (BB-37): Sunk-raised Dec. 28, 1943 never returned to service.
California (BB-44): Sunk-returned to service Jan. 31, 1944.
West Virginia (BB-48): Sunk-returned to service Sept. 14, 1944.
Colorado (BB-45): Was undergoing modernization at Puget Sound.
Maryland (BB-46): Damaged-returned to service Feb. 26,1942.
Utah (AG-16) (BB-31):Target ship, sunk—destroyed, never raised)

Atlantic Fleet

Texas (BB-35)	*New Mexico (BB-40)*
New York (BB-34)	*Wyoming* (AG-17) (BB-32)
Arkansas (BB-33)	Training ship.
Idaho (BB-42)	*North Carolina* (BB-55)
Missssissippi (BB-41)	*Washington* (BB-56)

December 8, 1941—Only nine (9) ships remained in active status, and only with the Atlantic fleet, one of those, *Wyoming* (AG-17/BB-32), was being used as and was suitable for use only as a training ship due to her earlier demilitarization in compliance with the Naval Treaties.

Following the destruction of *Arizona* (BB-39) and the Pacific Battleship Fleet's extreme loss at Pearl Harbor on December 7, and its consequent rebuild, many major naval engagements in both the Atlantic and Pacific were to be involved during the ensuing 1,365 days and the end of World War II in Tokyo Bay September 2, 1945, on board *Missouri* (BB 63).

1942 in the Atlantic

The older battleships were assigned convoy duty for protection of the transport ships while in transit to England and Russia with supplies. Also, the troop transports and supply ships headed for the first landings in North Africa.

November 8, 1942—*Massachusetts* (BB-59) engaged the French battleship *Jean Bart* at the Battle of Casablanca during the invasion of North Africa, and silenced the French battleship's only operational 15 inch gun turret.[14] *New York* (BB-34) and *Texas* (BB-35) were also involved in the invasion of North Africa offering fire support to the landing forces as requested.[15]

During 1942—*South Dakota* class of four ships were all commissioned. *South Dakota* (BB-57) on March 20, *Indiana* (BB-58) on April 30, *Massachusetts* (BB-59) on May 12, and *Alabama* (BB-60) on August 16.

1942 in the Pacific

Two days after the attack on Pearl Harbor *Idaho* (BB-42) and *Mississippi* (BB-41) were transferred from the Atlantic Fleet at Hvalfjordur, Iceland and arrived in San Francisco on January 31, 1942, via Norfolk and the Panama Canal.

Tennessee (BB-43), *Colorado* (BB-45), *Pennsylvania* (BB-38), and *Maryland* (BB-46) were used in the Pacific Fleet's defense line operating out of west coast ports during the early months of 1942 and several were in the area approximately 1200 miles northeast of the Hawaiian Islands during the Battle of Midway on June 5.[16]

North Carolina (BB-55) in an odd twist of fate, following the carrier *Wasp* (CV-7), was also torpedoed along with the destroyer *O'Brien* (DD-415) by the Japanese submarine *I-19* on September 15. *Wasp* (CV-7) was sunk as a result of being hit by three torpedoes, while *North Carolina* (BB-55), being hit by one torpedo, required repairs at Pearl Harbor due to the 18 feet high by 32 feet long hole in the hull on the port side abreast number one turret. After temporary repairs at Noumea, New Caledonia, and en route to the States *O'Brien* (DD-415) broke up and sank off Samoa on October 19 from the hull damage she suffered in the torpedoing.[17]

October 25 and 26, during the Battle of Santa Cruz while *South Dakota* (BB-57) was operating with the carriers *Hornet* (CV-8) and *Enterprise* (CV-6), at approximately 1230 hours on the 26th, *South Dakota* sustained a 500-pound bomb hit on top of her number one turret, with no personnel injuries noted.

Washington (BB-56) and *South Dakota* (BB-57) sailed out of Noumea, and on November 14 and 15, 1942, at the Battle of Savo Island, *South Dakota* (BB-57) had her fire control radar fail during the engagement. She had received 42 hits from three or more Japanese ships including the battleship *Kirishima*, with a loss of 38 crewmen killed and 60 wounded. Determining that she was no longer receiving enemy fire, *South Dakota* (BB-57) retired from the action, but *Washington* (BB-56) which was unobserved in the shadows behind *South Dakota* (BB-57), opened fire on *Kirishima* hitting her with nine 16 inch shell fire and about 40 five-inch shells causing heavy damage and loss of her steering gear.

Unable to steer, burning and exploding, *Kirishima* was later abandoned and scuttled on November 15.

Some of *South Dakota* (BB-57) battle damage was repaired at Noumea, then she went on to the New York Navy Yard arriving December 18, 1942.

1943 in the Atlantic

South Dakota (BB-57), repaired at New York following the damage received during the engagement with *Kirishima*, was in the Atlantic operating with the carrier *Ranger* (CV-4) until mid-April, then with the recently completed *Alabama* (BB-60) was assigned to the British Home Fleet Base at Scapa Flow for convoy duty protecting convoys to Britain and Russia.

Arkansas (BB-33) and *Texas* (BB-35) also served convoy duty operating out of various east coast ports. *New York* (BB-34) became a training ship in Chesapeake Bay, training gunners for battleships and destroyer escorts.[18]

Completing their assigned convoy escort duties in August, *Alabama* (BB-60) and *South Dakota* (BB-57) were both transferred to the Pacific.

1943 in the Pacific

May 4, and operations began for retaking the Aleutian Islands with *Pennsylvania* (BB-38) as flagship of the taskforce.

August 15 during the final assault on Kiska with fire support action provided by *Tennessee* (BB-43).[19]

North Carolina (BB-55) supported the landings of June 30 on New Georgia.[20]

Massachusetts (BB-59), *Indiana* (BB-58) and *North Carolina* (BB-55) were all with the fast carrier forces on November 19 as anti-aircraft fire support escorts for the raids on Makin and again later for the air strikes on Kwajelein.[21]

Invasion of the Gilbert Islands began on November 20, 1943, with fire support provided the Fifth Amphibious Force with *Pennsylvania* (BB-38) as flagship.[22]

Also on November 20 *Tennessee* (BB-43), *Maryland* (BB-46) and *Colorado* (BB-45) were off Tarawa.[23]

1944 in the Atlantic

June 6, D-Day began with *Nevada* (BB-36) stationed at Utah Beach as one of the fire support ships, with *Texas* (BB-35) and *Arkansas* (BB-33) fulfilling the same duties at Omaha Beach.[24]

On June 25, *Texas* (BB-35) while providing fire support for the troops while they were engaged in the taking of Cherbourg, France, was hit by an 11-inch shell fire from a coastal battery that struck the top of the armored conning tower demolishing her bridge and killing the helmsman.[25]

Texas (BB-35) and *Nevada* (BB-36) along with *Arkansas* (BB-33) also participated with the landing fire support for the invasion of Southern France beginning on August 15.[26]

With the European Theater drawing to a close and there being greatly reduced requirements for American ships in the Atlantic, four additional ships were transferred to Pacific. They were *Nevada* (BB-36), *Texas* (BB-35), *New York* (BB-34), and *Arkansas* (BB-33). This transfer put all of the American battleships in the Pacific except for *Wyoming* (BB-32/AG-17), which was serving as a gunnery training ship. These transfers began in October and were completed in December.

1944 in the Pacific

The "fast battleships" now numbered eight with *Alabama* (BB-60), *Iowa* (BB-61), *New Jersey* (BB-62), *Indiana* (BB-58), *North Carolina* (BB-55), *Washington* (BB-56), *South Dakota* (BB-57), and *Massachusetts* (BB-59). They were on hand for the January 29 invasion of the Marshall Islands. They were then assigned among the carriers of the battle groups to provide the anti-aircraft fire support.[27]

Invasion landing fire support duties at Kwajalein were assigned to *Pennsylvania* (BB-38), *Tennessee* (BB-43), and *Colorado* (BB-45).[28]

On February 1, during the early morning blackness off Kwajelein, *Washington* (BB-56) rammed *Indiana* (BB-58) as she cut across *Washington's* (BB-56) bow while dropping out of formation to refuel escorting destroyers, causing both to be retired to fleet operations at Pearl for repairs. *Washington* (BB-56) continued on to Puget Sound to have a new bow fitted. Both were subsequently out of action for several months.

February 17-18, saw the "fast battleships" including *Iowa* (BB-61) and *New Jersey* (BB-62) as they participated in the raids on Truk.

March 18, while participating in the bombardments of Mille Atoll, *Iowa* (BB-61) was hit by two 4.7 inch shells from shore batteries but suffered no serious damage.[29]

June and the "fast battleships" including *North Carolina* (BB-55), *Washington* (BB-56), *South Dakota* (BB-57), *Indiana* (BB-58), *Alabama* (BB-60), *Iowa* (BB-61), and *New Jersey* (BB-62) were participating in a defensive position west of the Marianas to protect the invasion force in the Marianas and subsequently in the Battle of the Philippine Sea, the "Great Marianas Turkey Shoot" of June 19, 1944, providing the carriers with the successful anti-aircraft fire support. *South Dakota* (BB-57) was hit with a 500 pound bomb on the main deck by an aircraft attack from the Japanese aircraft headed for the American carriers where she suffered the loss of 24 crewmen killed and 27 wounded. *Indiana* (BB-58) also suffered a near miss from two torpedoes during the course of the battle.[30] Invasion of the Marianas on June 15 began with fire support duty including *Tennessee* (BB-43), *California* (BB-44), *Maryland* (BB-46), and *Colorado* (BB-45).[31]

July 19, 1944, and *Tennessee* (BB-43), *California* (BB-44), *Colorado* (BB-45), and other ships of the bombardment force participated in the bombardments and fire support duties off Guam. On July 23, they were again together off Tinian, continuing until August 2.[32]

Maryland (BB-46) was one of the several older battleships which participated in the conquest of Palau during September 13 and 14, 1944.[33]

The "fast battleships" were included with the carrier raids on the Japanese-held perimeter surrounding the Philippine Sea which included the Philippines and the Carolines during September.[34]

The landings at Leyte Gulf beginning on October 18 were covered by units including *Tennessee* (BB-43), *California* (BB-44), and *Pennsylvania* (BB-38).[35]

During the late hours of October 24th and early hours of October 25th the last battle of battleship versus battleship occurred during the Battle of Surigao Strait when the American battle force consisting of *West Virginia* (BB-48), *Tennessee* (BB-43), *California* (BB-44), *Maryland* (BB-46), *Mississippi* (BB-41) and *Pennsylvania* (BB-38) engaged the Japanese battle force that also included the Japanese battleships *Fuso* and *Yamashiro*. Both *Fuso* and *Yamashiro* were sunk during the engagement.

In Leyte Gulf on November 27, *Colorado* (BB-45) was hit twice by kamikaze attacks killing 19 and wounding 72 of her crew with moderate damage. Also, on November 29, *Maryland* (BB-46) was hit between number (1) and (2) turrets, killing 31 and wounding 1 officer and 29

additional crewmen, resulting in serious damage requiring major repair at Pearl Harbor.[36]

December 15, *West Virginia* (BB-48) as flagship was in action with the bombardments conducted at Mindoro.[37]

1945 in the Atlantic

Wyoming (BB-32/AG-17) continued her gunnery training drills which she had begun in February 1942.

1945 in the Pacific

All of the American battleships were now in the Pacific, including the new "fast battleships" *New Jersey* (BB-62), *Missouri* (BB-63), and *Wisconsin* (BB-64) which had just recently arrived following commissioning and trials. These, with the noted exception of *Wyoming* (AG-17/BB-32), were busy grouping into their respective carrier and troop landing support forces.

Off Luzon on January 6, *New Mexico* (BB-40) was hit on the bridge by a kamikaze killing her commanding officer Captain R.W. Fleming and 29 other crewmen, also wounding 87 more, with minimal ship's damage, while at Lingayen Gulf *California's* (BB-44) damage was more serious, with 44 of her crew killed and 155 wounded, all of which later required repair at Puget Sound.[38]

Also off Luzon on January 6, *Mississippi* (BB-41) was hit near the waterline by a kamikaze and on January 9 in Lingayen Gulf.

Colorado (BB-45) sustained a hit from accidental gun fire to her superstructure killing 19 and wounding 51 of her crew. Neither were required to retire from the battle line for damage repair until after their actions were completed.

Tennessee (BB-43) and six other older battleships including *Arkansas* (BB-33), the oldest battleship in the Fleet, along with the two "fast battleships" *North Carolina* (BB-55) and *Washington* (BB-56) saw action at Iwo Jima from February 16 thru 19.[39]

March 27 off Okinawa, *Nevada* (BB-36) was hit by a kamikaze and suffered main battery turret damage and eleven crewmen were killed. Two additional crewmen were killed on April 5 when she was also hit by fire from a shore battery.

April 1 off Okinawa, *West Virginia* (BB-48) sustained a kamikaze hit on her superstructure just forward of the secondary fire director number 2 with four crewmen killed and seven wounded.[40]

April 7 at Okinawa, *Maryland* (BB-46) hit on side of number 3 turret by a kamikaze plane carrying a 500-pound bomb with 10 killed, 6 missing, and 37 more crewmen injured. She did not retire from the firing line until April 14. The sustained damage required time at Puget Sound for repair and she was then out of action until war was over.[41]

April 11, also off Okinawa, *Missouri* (BB-63) was hit by a kamikaze just below her main deck on the starboard side with little damage. On April 16 she also was the victim of a hit on her stern crane, again with very little damage.[42]

April 12, *Tennessee* (BB-43) was hit along the superstructure ending near turret (3) with 22 crewmen killed or mortally wounded and 107 injured.[43]

April 14, *New York* (BB-34) was grazed by a kamikaze which demolished her spotting plane on its catapult off Okinawa.

May 12, *New Mexico* (BB-40) in Hagushi anchorage was attacked by two kamikaze. One plunged into her, the other hit her with his bomb. These hits caused the loss of 54 crewmen killed and 119 more wounded. She sailed to Leyte for damage repair on May 28.

June 5, *Mississippi* (BB-41) was hit on her starboard side off Okinawa with little noted damage.

During July and August, the "fast battleships" were with the carriers for raids on the Japanese "Home Islands." *South Dakota* (BB-57), *Indiana* (BB-58), and *Massachusetts* (BB-59) shelled the Kamaishi Iron Works on July 14 and the aircraft factory at Hamatsu on July 29th.[44]

August 9, 1945, *Massachusetts* (BB-59) fired what was probably the last 16 inch shell fired in combat during World War II at the Kamaishi, Honshu, Japan during bombardment of the "Home Islands."

This is also the day the second atomic bomb of World War II was dropped on Nagasaki, Japan.[44]

August 12 in Buckner Bay, Okinawa, *Pennsylvania* (BB-38) received torpedo damage to the starboard stern quarter inflicting serious damage, killing 20 crewmen and wounding 10 more. This damage took her out of the war. She was towed to Guam for temporary repairs, then she went on to Bremerton for repair work under greatly reduced power.[45]

September 2, 1945, five of the old battleships and five of the new "fast battleships" were anchored in Tokyo Bay for the Japanese surrender ceremonies. The "old battleships" were represented by *New Mexico* (BB-40), *Mississippi* (BB-41), *Idaho* (BB-42), *Colorado* (BB-45), and *West Virginia* (BB-48), a fitting tribute to a rebuilt survivor of the Pearl Harbor attack. The "fast battleships" were represented by *Missouri* (BB-63), the site of the signing of the ceremonies, *South Dakota* (BB-57), *Washington* (BB-56), *Alabama* (BB-60), and *Iowa* (BB-61).

September 3, 1945:
Battleships in Active Service (total: 24)

"Old Battleships"=14

Wyoming (BB-32/AG-17)	*Tennessee* (BB-43)
Arkansas (BB-33)	*California* (BB-44)
New York (BB-34)	*Colorado* (BB-45)
Texas (BB-35)	*Maryland* (BB-46)
Nevada (BB-36)	*West Virginia* (BB-48)
Pennsylvania (BB-38)	**"War Losses"**
New Mexico (BB-40)	*Utah* (BB-31/AG-16)
Mississippi (BB-41)	*Oklahoma* (BB-37)
Idaho (BB-42)	*Arizona* (BB-39)

"Fast Battleships"=10

North Carolina (BB-55)	*Alabama* (BB-60)
Washington (BB-56)	*Iowa* (BB-61)
South Dakota (BB-57)	*New Jersey* (BB-62)
Indiana (BB-58)	*Missouri* (BB-63)
Massachusetts (BB-59)	*Wisconsin* (BB-64)

February 15, 1946, *Mississippi* (BB-41) was decommissioned as a battleship and converted to the test and training ship (AG-128/EAG-128) and served in the Operational Deployment Force.

On July 1 and July 25, 1946, the first American Pacific atom bomb tests were conducted at Bikini Atoll in the Pacific. These tests were designated the "Able" and "Baker" tests. Four of the "old battleships" were used as target ships during these tests along with many other older and World War II prize ships. The battleships used were *Arkansas* (BB-33), *New York* (BB-34), *Nevada* (BB-36), and *Pennsylvania* (BB-38).

Arkansas (BB-33) sank as a result of "Baker Test" on July 25, 1946, along with several other ships.

On May 17, 1947, following her sale to Moore Drydock Co. of Oakland, California, *Oklahoma* (BB-37), which had seen no further action in World War II following her damage at Pearl Harbor on December 7, 1941, parted her tow line and sank 540 miles out of Pearl Harbor bound for San Francisco.

September 16, 1947, *Wyoming* (AG-17/BB-32), was stricken from the Navy list to be sold for scrapping.

October 13, 1947, *New Mexico* (BB-40), was stricken from the Navy list and sold for scrapping.

November 24, 1947, *Idaho* (BB-42), was stricken from the Navy list and sold for scrapping.

February 10, 1948, *Pennsylvania* (BB-38) was scuttled off Kwajalein Island after the conclusion of tests conducted following the atom bomb tests July 1 and July 25, 1946.

April 30, 1948, the first complete battleship to be permanently dedicated as a memorial was established with *Texas* (BB-35) being placed at San Jacinto Park, La Porte, Texas. Prior to this the *Maine* (BB-00/ACR-1) memorial was established in New York City on May 28, 1913. The *Oregon* (BB-03) was used as a "floating monument and museum at Portland, Oregon between June 1925 and November 2, 1942. She was eventually returned to the Navy during World War II. (Please see the individual ships data sheets for her final disposition.)

July 8, 1948 *New York* (BB-34) was sunk 40 miles out from Pearl Harbor during an eight hour battle maneuver test, after conclusion of tests conducted following the atom bomb tests.

July 31, 1948 *Nevada* (BB-36) was sunk off Hawaii during Naval gunfire and aerial torpedo tests, after conclusion of tests conducted following the atom bomb tests.

1950 Battleships in Active Service: Missouri (BB-63)

Pacific Reserve Fleet	Atlantic Reserve Fleet
Indiana (BB-58)	*Iowa* (BB-61)
Alabama (BB-60)	*Massachusetts* (BB-59)
Colorado (BB-45)	*New Jersey* (BB-62)
Maryland (BB-46)	*Wisconsin* (BB-64)
West Virginia (BB-48)	*Washington* (BB-56)
	California (BB-44)
	Tennessee (BB-43)
	South Dakota (BB-57)
	North Carolina (BB-55)

March 7, 1950, Admiral Arthur W. Radford, Commander in Chief of the Pacific Fleet, issued an official order: "From today on the *USS Arizona* (BB-39) will again fly our country's flag just as proudly as she did on the morning of December 7, 1941. I am sure the *Arizona*'s crew will know and appreciate what we are doing".[46]

January 17, 1950, and the *Missouri* (BB-63) while leaving her home port of Hampton Roads, ran aground at a point 1.6 miles from the Thimble Shoals Light. She was finally freed on February 1 with the aid of tugs, pontoons, and an incoming tide.

June 25, 1950, and the Korean War began with the crossing of the border between North and South Korea by the North Koreans in a massed surprise attack.

Missouri (BB-63) arrived there on September 14 for her first of two tours of duty providing fire support for the army, marines, and the Republic of Korea's land forces. The first was completed on March 19, 1951, and the second commenced on October 19, 1952, and ran until March 25, 1953.

Iowa (BB-61), *New Jersey* (BB-62), and *Wisconsin* (BB-64) were all recommissioned during 1951 and each also saw action in shore bombardment and troop support. *Iowa* (BB-61) completed one tour of duty, from April 8 to October 16, 1952. *New Jersey* (BB-62) completed two tours of duty, with the first from May 17, 1951, to November 13, 1951, and the second from April 6, 1953, to July 26, 1953.

Wisconsin (BB-64) completed only one tour of duty from October 26, 1951 to March 19, 1952. But while on this tour of duty she was the only battleship to be hit by enemy gunfire during the "Conflict." On March 15, 1952, she was hit by a 155-millimeter (6.10-inch) gun battery off Songjin, Korea, on the shield of a starboard 40-millimeter gun mount. Following this hit, she blasted the gun battery with a 16-inch gun salvo, and the enemy battery ceased to exist.

All were decommissioned during late 1950s. When *Wisconsin* (BB-64) decommissioned on March 8, 1958, the United States Navy was without an active battleship since *Texas* (BB-000) was the first to commission on August 15, 1895.

On May 16, 1958, the battleship *Arizona* (BB-39) memorial was officially authorized by Congress to be constructed at Pearl Harbor, Honolulu, Hawaii. This step followed Admiral Radford's lead demonstrated on March 7, 1950.

February 24, 1959, *California* (BB-44) and *Maryland* (BB-46) were stricken from the Navy list to be sold for scrapping.

March 1, 1959, *Tennessee* (BB-43), *Colorado* (BB-45) and *West Virginia* (BB-48) were stricken from the Navy list to be sold for scrapping.

1960 active battleships (none)

Atlantic Reserve Fleet	Pacific Reserve Fleet
North Carolina (BB-55)	*Indiana* (BB-58)
Washington (BB-56)	*Alabama* (BB-60)
South Dakota (BB-57)	*Missouri* (BB-63)
Massachusetts (BB-59)	
New Jersey (BB-62)	
Iowa (BB-61)	
Wisconsin (BB-64)	

June 1, 1960, *Washington* (BB-56) was stricken from the Navy list to be sold for scrap.

April 29, 1962, the *North Carolina* (BB-55) battleship memorial was dedicated at Wilmington, North Carolina. "A memorial to all of the men and women of North Carolina who had served in the United States Armed Forces during World War II, and to the memory of nearly 10,000 North Carolinians who gave their lives in that war."[47]

June 1, 1962, *Indiana* (BB-58) and *South Dakota* (BB-57) stricken from the Navy list to be sold for scrapping. A memorial with artifacts from *South Dakota* (BB-57) was dedicated September 7, 1969, in Sioux Falls, South Dakota.

January 9, 1965, the *Alabama* (BB-60) battleship memorial was dedicated at Mobile, Alabama.

August 14, 1965, the *Massachusetts* (BB-59) battleship memorial was dedicated at Fall River, Massachusetts.

April 6, 1968 the *New Jersey* (BB-62) was recommissioned from the Atlantic Reserve Fleet in order to provide shore bombardment and fire support missions for the ground forces serving in Vietnam.

She arrived off the coast of Vietnam on September 30, 1968, and except for replenishment of her stores and munitions, she performed her prescribed duties until leaving on April 3, 1969.

While preparing for her second tour of duty, she was again placed on the inactive list and subsequently decommissioned at the Puget Sound Naval Shipyard on December 17, 1969.

1970 active battleships (none)

Atlantic Reserve Fleet	Pacific Reserve Fleet
Iowa (BB-61)	*Missouri* (BB-63)
Wisconsin (BB-64)	*New Jersey* (BB-62)

During the late 1970s, discussions were held concerning the size and makeup of the U.S. Navy, with comments on the possible recommissioning of the *Iowas*.

1980 active battleships (none)

Atlantic Reserve Fleet	**Pacific Reserve Fleet**
Iowa (BB-61)	*Missouri* (BB-63)
Wisconsin (BB-64)	*New Jersey* (BB-62)

Following world political conditions and the growing strength of the Soviet Navy in capital ship development, the decision to reactivate the four *Iowas* was made. Each ship was to be fully refitted and also were upgraded to use the fuel oil of the current fleet in place of the fuel oils they were originally designed for, due to its obsolescence. They were also updated with the newest radars and armed with Tomahawk cruise missiles, Harpoon Anti-Ship missiles and Phalanx guns. *New Jersey* (BB-62) was the first reactivated and she was recommissioned on December 28, 1982.

From September 1983 to early 1984, *New Jersey* was off the coast of Beirut, Lebanon, to provide the U.S. Marines with fire support.[48]

Iowa (BB-61) recommissioned on April 28, 1984, followed by *Missouri* (BB-63) on July 1, 1986, and *Wisconsin* (BB-64) on October 22, 1988.

On April 19, 1989, *Iowa* (BB-61), while cruising northeast of Puerto Rico performing gunfire support exercise, the middle gun of number two turret had the propellant powder charge explode, killing forty-seven men of the gun crew. Following several complete investigations, no clear final explanation of the tragic accident has yet come forth.[49]

1990 active battleships (four)

Iowa (BB-61)	*Missouri* (BB-63)
New Jersey (BB-62)	*Wisconsin* (BB-64)

Even though the ships were performing their duties well, it was again decided to deactivate the battleships and on October 26, 1990, upon completion of repairs following the turret explosion on the *Iowa* (BB-61) she was laid up and decommissioned at the Philadelphia Naval Shipyard.[50]

August 2, 1990, began with the Iraqi invasion of Kuwait, followed on August 7 with the beginning of Operation Desert Shield. *Wisconsin* (BB-64) was there at the beginning. She served the complete Operation Desert Shield campaign to January 14, 1991. *Missouri* (BB-63) arrived to support Operation Desert Shield in early January 1991.[51]

Operation Desert Storm began in the early morning hours of January 15, 1991, with the massive air strike against Iraq. Both *Wisconsin* (BB-64) and *Missouri* (BB-63) launched their cruise missiles and provided shore bombardment of Iraqi positions in Kuwait. Each performed its assigned missions well and was there till the operation ended with the completion of Operation Desert Storm on February 27, 1991.[51]

While *Wisconsin* (BB-64) and *Missouri* (BB-63) were active in Operation Desert Storm, *New Jersey* (BB-62) was decommissioned for the fourth time on February 8, 1991, at Long Beach, California.

On September 30, 1991, *Wisconsin* (BB-64) was also decommissioned at the Philadelphia Naval Yard.

Missouri (BB-63) participated at the 50th anniversary ceremonies commemorating the Japanese attack on Pearl Harbor on December 7, 1991, then proceeded on to Bremerton where she was the last to decommission on March 31, 1992.

1994 active battleships (none)

Atlantic Reserve Fleet	**Pacific Reserve Fleet**
Iowa (BB-61)	*New Jersey* (BB-62)
Wisconsin (BB-64)	*Missouri* (BB-63)

1995 significant events

January 12, 1995, *Iowa* (BB-61), *New Jersey* (BB-62), *Missouri* (BB-63) and *Wisconsin* (BB-64) stricken from the Navy list, awaiting final disposition.

....

American Battleship Fleet Anchorages (1895–1992)

U.S. East Coast
Hampton Roads, Virginia
Norfolk, Virginia

U.S. West Coast
San Pedro/Long Beach, California—after 1919[52]
San Diego, California—before 1919[52]
San Francisco, California—before 1919
Seattle, Washington—before 1919

Pacific
Pearl Harbor, Hawaii—after 1940

Foreign Soils
Guantanamo Bay, Cuba
Subic Bay, Philippines—after 1945 to 1992

Naval & Private Construction Yards (1895–1958)

U.S. East Coast
New York Navy Yard, Brooklyn, New York
Norfolk Navy Yard, Portsmouth, Virginia
William Cramp & Sons, Philadelphia, Pennsylvania
Newport News Shipbuilding Co., Newport News, Virginia
Bath Iron Works, Bath, Maine
Fore River Co., Quincy, Massachusetts
New York Shipbuilding Co., Camden, New Jersey
Philadelphia Navy Yard, Philadelphia, Pennsylvania
Bethlehem Steel Co., Quincy, Massachusetts

U.S. West Coast
Union Iron Works, San Francisco, California
Moran Brothers, Seattle, Washington
Mare Island Navy Yard, Vallejo, California

"Baker Day" atomic bomb test, Bikini Atoll, July 25, 1946. Frame 7 of a series of ground level views, taken about six seconds after detonation. Identifiable ships are (l–r): P*ennsylvania* (BB-38), *New York* (BB-35), *Salt Lake City* (CA-26), *Nagato* (ex-Japanese BB), *Nevada* (BB-36). Dark area on right side of water column marks the location of *Arkansas* (BB-33). *Arkansas* sank as a result of this test.

EPILOGUE

POSSIBLE FUTURE OF THE SHIPS? Perhaps additional recommissionings? They rest majestically at anchor, properly preserved by their former crewmen, awaiting their next call for future history.

If the ships are never recalled to duty, it has been long thought and suggested that at least two of the Iowas would end their long and illustrious careers by becoming memorials as some of their earlier sisters have.

Missouri (BB-63) has already served in somewhat that capacity during her period of decommissioning at Bremerton, Washington from 1955 to 1986.

When it was considered during the early 1970's to possibly scrap the Iowas, people in the state of New Jersey were beginning to make plans to acquire *New Jersey* (BB-62) and place her as a Memorial.

Wisconsin (BB-64) and *Iowa* (BB-61), only history will tell.

A LOOK AT HISTORY AND the most recognized American Battleship names.

Maine (BB-00/ACR-1)—Lost by explosion in Havana, Cuba harbor on February 15, 1898. Remembered as the ignition point for the Spanish-American War.

Arizona (BB-39)—Lost in the Japanese attack on Pearl Harbor, Hawaii on December 7, 1941. Remembered as the attack that took the United States into World War II.

Missouri (BB-63)—Remembered as the site in Tokyo Bay, Tokyo, Japan for the signing of the Japanese surrender document, formally ending World War II on September 2, 1945, and as the third ship of the Iowa class. Perhaps, and history will tell, the last American and the world's last active duty battleship.

Iowa (BB-61)—for class name of the last completed American battleship, with a total active and inactive service life of 51 years. Being first commissioned on February 22, 1943, the lead ship of the six ship Iowa class.

FINALLY, A LOOK AT INTERESTING points of history on several of the other battleships.

Oregon (BB-03)—after being recalled from the State of Oregon from its place of honor as a floating museum and memorial, and partial scrapping for its steel during World War II, the ship served as a floating munitions ship as IX-22. This configuration lasted until March 1, 1956.

Kearsarge (BB-05)—following decommissioning as a battleship, she was converted to a crane ship, *Crane Ship 1*, and served in this capacity until June 22, 1955.

Illinois (BB-07)—fitted out as a floating armory, when excluded from further use as a battleship by terms of the Washington Naval Treaty of February 8, 1922. She served in this capacity until December 31, 1955. Her name was changed to *Prairie State* and designated (IX-15) on January 8, 1941 when the name was assigned to the new battleship *Illinois* (BB-65), number five of the six ship *Iowa* class.

United States Naval Ordnances
Battleships (1895–1994)

Guns were built at the Washington gun factory,
proved at Indian Head, Indiana, Dahlgren, Virginia and the Potomac Ranges.

Type	Bore in Inches	Model	Length in Caliber	Weight of A.P. shell in lbs.	Initial Shell Velocity Ft./Sec	Maximum Shell Range Yards
HEAVY [53]	18		48	(Designed-Never Built)		42500+
[53]	16		56	(Designed-Never Built)		42500+
	16	MK-7	50	2700	2500	42500
	16	MK-6	45	2700	2300	36900
	16	MK-1	45	2100	2800	34500
	14	MK-4	50	1400	2800	34000
[54]	14	MK-8	45	1500	2600	23000
[55]	14	MK-3	45	1400	2600	18000
[56]	14	MK-1	45	1400	2700	24000
[57]	13	MK-1 & 2	35	1130	2000	16000+
[58]	12	MK-7	50	870	2950	16000
	12	MK-6	45	870	2850	15000
	12	MK-5	45	870	2700	15000
	12	MK-3 & 4	40	870	2600	14000
	12	MK-1 & 2	35	870	2100	12000
	10	MK-3	40	510	2700	15000
	10	MK-1 & 2	30	510	2000	11000
MEDIUM	8	MK-6	45	260	2750	12000
	8	MK-5	40	260	2500	10000
	8	MK-3 & 4	35	260	2100	8000+
	6		52			12000+
[54]	6	MK-8	50	105	2800	12000
[55]	6	MK-6	50	105	2600	10000
[56]	6	MK-9	45	105	2250	8000+
[57]	6	MK-4 &7	40	105	2150	8000+
[57]	5	MK-13	51	50	3150	12000
	5	MK-12	51	50	3150	12000
	5	MK-7	51	50	3150	12000
	5	MK-6	50	50	3000	10000
	5	MK-5 & 6	50	50	2700	8000+
	5	MK-2,3 & 4	40	50	2300	8000+
LIGHT	4	MK-8	50	33	2800	10000+
	4	MK-7	50	33	2500	10000+
[54]	4	MK-5 & 6	40	33	2000	10000+
[55]	4	MK-2 & 3	40	33	2000	10000+
[56]	3	MK-21	50	13	2700	14600
[57]	3 (AA)	MK-10	50	13	2700	10000+
[58]	3	MK-5 & 6	50	13	2700	10000+
	3 (AA)	S-A	50	13	2700	10000+
	3	MK-2 & 3	50	13	2700	10000+
AA [59]	40mm	MK-1 & 2		2.0	2890	11000
[60]	1.10"/75	MK-1		.92	2700	7400
[61]						
	20mm	MK-4		.92	2740	4800
	20mm	CIWS (Phalanx)[59]		650 gns	3700	11700
MISSILES	Tomahawk (TLAN-Mode)[59]					Max 1500 N-Miles
	Harpoon (BOL-Mode)[59]					Max 85 N-Miles

INDIVIDUAL SHIP DATA SHEETS

....

THE INDIVIDUAL SHIP DATA SHEETS list a very condensed version of the available technical data and operational history of each ship. But all of the information concerning congressional authorization date, keel laying, commissioning date, the ship's first commanding officer, and the technical data for the ship's machinery and weaponry as listed for her first commissioning are listed.

Early ships from the first *Maine* (BB-00) up to *Florida* (BB-30) did not appear to change much during their careers. This is most likely due to the early evolutionary changes, leading to the shorter life span of the ships.

The later ships from *Utah* (BB-31) up to *California* (BB-48) changed more radically as they were upgraded and rebuilt as a result of the Washington and London Naval Conferences, and of course World War II.

Ships built just before and during World War II, *North Carolina* (BB-55) to *Wisconsin* (BB-64), were also rebuilt and repaired for any battle damage. The ships *North Carolina* (BB-55) through *Alabama* (BB-60) had relatively short active duty lives, from five to seven years, then spending up to fourteen years in the reserve fleets before being deemed obsolete and transferred into a place of honor as a memorial, or specific items salvaged and then put to the cutter's torch.

Where possible the data sheets show some of the many upgrades in the (bracketed) information. This information was used with permission from the noted sources.

Of course the four *Iowa*s are back in the reserve fleets, awaiting their history.

Left: *Connecticut* leading the Atlantic Fleet to sea, circa December, 1907, probably at the start of the cruise around the world of the "Great White Fleet." NH 100349

Unless noted, all photographs in this book were obtained from the U.S. Naval Historical Center

USS Maine
ex-ACR-1

1st Commanding Officer: Captain A. S. Crowninshield
Authorized: August 3, 1886
Keel Laid: October 17, 1888
Launched: November 18, 1889
Commissioned: September 17, 1895
Sponsor: Miss Alice Tracy Wilmerding
Displacement Standard Tons: 6682
Displacement Full Load Tons:
Design Crew Complement: 31 officers, 343 enlisted
Main Guns: 4-10" 35 caliber, 6-6" 40 caliber
Secondary Guns: 7-6 pounder, 8-1 pounder
Construction Costs: $2,500,000 maximum
Armor: Maximum thickness 12" at turret face plates
Length Overall: 319'
Mean Draught: 21'6"
Extreme Beam: 57'
Torpedo Tubes: 4-14" surface
Catapults: None
Builder: New York Navy Yard, Brooklyn, New York
Original Engines Manufactured: Quintard Iron Works; type: vertical, triple expansion, reciprocating
Original Boilers Manufactured: Quintard Iron Works; type: FT; no. 4
Original Fuel: Coal, 896 tons
Drive: Reciprocating, 2 screws
Sisters: *Maine* Class Battleship Prototype
Designed Speed: 17 knots
Designed Shaft Horsepower: 9000
Design Comments:
· No. 1 in battleship prototypes—second class battleship—heavy armored cruiser
· Sea-going double-bottomed armored vessel

History Highlights:
· ex-ACR-1
· Training cruises and East Coast operations 1895–1897
· Dec. 16, 1897 assigned to North Atlantic Squadron
· Normal refits and overhauls
· Arrived Havana, Cuba, Jan. 25, 1898
· Sunk Havana, Cuba, 2140 hours, Feb. 15, 1898, with 252 on board killed or missing
Date Decommissioned:
Final Disposition: Hulk refloated Feb. 2, 1912, towed to Gulf of Mexico, sunk with honors, March 16, 1912

Maine, being scuttled with honors off Havana, Cuba in the Gulf of Mexico on March 16, 1912. NH 46791

Maine, photo of her wreck, in Havana Harbor on Feb. 16, 1898, the morning after the explosion. NH 46776

Maine. Photo taken sometime between her commissioning on Sept. 17, 1895 and her loss on Feb. 15, 1898. (First American prototype battleship.) NH 60255

1st Commanding Officer: Capt. H. Glass

Authorized: August 8, 1886

Keel Laid: June 1, 1889

Launched: June 28. 1892

Commissioned: August 15, 1895

Sponsor: Miss Madge Houston Williams

Displacement Standard Tons: 6315

Displacement Full Load Tons:

Design Crew Complement: 30 officers, 362 enlisted

Main Guns: 2-12"I 35 caliber, 6-6" 40 caliber

Secondary Guns: 12-6 pounder 6-1 pounder 4-37 millimeter

Construction Costs: $2,500,000 maximum

Armor: Maximum thickness 12" at turret face plates

Length Overall: 308' 10"

Mean Draught: 22'6"

Extreme Beam: 64'1"

Torpedo Tubes: 4-14" surface

Catapults: None

Builder: Norfolk Navy Yard, Portsmouth, Virginia

Original Engines Manufactured: Richmond Locomotive Works; vertical inverted direct acting triple expansion reciprocating.

Original Boilers Manufactured: Richmond Locomotive Works; type: FT; no. 4

Original Fuel: Coal, 850 tons

Drive: Reciprocating, 2 screws

Sisters: *Texas* Class Battleship Prototype

Designed Speed: 17 knots

Designed Shaft Horsepower: 8600

Design Comments:

· Sea-going double-bottomed armored vessel

· No. 2 in Battleship Prototypes

· Second-class Battleship—heavy armored cruiser

History Highlights:

• Cruise Atlantic coast 1895–1897; May 21, 1898 U.S. Flying Squadron off Cienfuegos, Cuba

• June 16, 1898 bombardment in Guantanamo Bay, Cuba

· July 3, 1898 Battle of Santiago de Cuba with Flying Squadron

• Dec. 2, 1898 Atlantic Fleet at Hampton Roads—cruising to Cuba also during 1898 and 1899

• Decommissioned 1901 for repair at Norfolk recommended Nov. 3, 1902

• Flagship of Atlantic Coast Squadron 1902–1905, with Atlantic Fleet till 1908

• Station ship at Charleston, S.C. 1908–1911

• Feb. 15, 1911 name changed to *San Marcos* to permit name to be assigned to USS *Texas* (BB-35)

Date Decommissioned: Oct. 10, 1911 and struck from Navy list

Final Disposition: Sunk as target ship in Tangier Sound in Chesapeake Bar in March, 1911

Texas, photo taken sometime during her active commissioned status 1895–1911. (Second American prototype battleship.) NH 63506

THE SAN MARCOS AFTER BEINC USED AS A

San Marcos (ex-*Texas*) after being used as a target ship in Chesapeake Bay, by *New Hampshire* (BB-25), in March, 1911. Note the numerous shell holes in the ship, which has settled to the bottom as a result of her damages. *Mohawk* (YT-17) is in the foreground. NH 73107

USS Indiana
BB-01

1st Commanding Officer: Captain R. D. Evans
Authorized: June 30, 1890
Keel Laid: May 7, 1891
Launched: Feb. 28, 1893
Commissioned: Nov. 20, 1895
Sponsor: Miss Jessie Miller
Displacement Standard Tons: 10,288
Design Crew Complement: 32 officers, 441 enlisted
Main Guns: 4-13" 35 caliber; 8-8" 35 caliber; 4-6" 40 caliber
Secondary Guns: 20-6 pounder; 6-1 pounder
Construction Costs: $4 million maximum plus armament
Armor: Maximum thickness 18" at turret face plates
Length Overall: 350'11"
Mean Draught: 24', 28' maximum
Extreme Beam: 69'3"
Torpedo Tubes: 6-18" surface
Catapults: none
Builder: William Cramp & Sons, Philadelphia
Original Engines Manufactured: Cramp type: vertical inverted triple expansion 3 cylinder reciprocating
Original Boilers Manufactured: Cramp type: FT; no. 6
Original Fuel: Coal, 1640 tons
Drive: Reciprocating, 2 screws
Sisters: *Indiana* class
Designed Speed: 15 knots
Designed Shaft Horsepower: 9000
Design Comments: sea going coast-line Battleship
History Highlights:
- 1895 Atlantic Fleet, 1898; part of Admiral Sampson's Squadron to Cuba
- May 12, 1898 shelled San Juan; June 1, 1898 blockade of Santiago, Cuba
- July 3, 1898 Battle of Santiago de Cuba
- Training and fleet exercises after the war
- Dec. 29, 1903 decommissioned; Jan. 6, 1906 recommissioned at New York Navy Yard; May 23, 1914 decommissioned at Philadelphia
- Recommissioned May 24, 1917 for WWI as training ship for gun crews
- Jan. 13, 1919 decommissioned at Philadelphia; reclassified as Coast BB-1 for name to new *Indiana* BB-50 March 29, 1919
Date Decommissioned: Oct. 14–Nov. 1, 1920 sunk at Tangier Sound in the Chesapeake Bay during critical aerial bomb tests
Commendations: None
Final Disposition: Hulk sold for scrap March 19, 1924

Indiana during the Fleet Review off New York City following the end of the Spanish-American war, 1898. NH 63503

Indiana and other ships, photographed on Nov. 18, 1919 at the Philadelphia Navy Yard. Front row, left to right: *Missouri* (BB-11), one ship of the *Connecticut* (BB-18) Class, *Michigan* (BB-27), and *St. Louis* (CA-20). Back row: *Maine* (BB-10), *Kentucky* (BB-6), *Kearsarge* (BB-5), *Indiana* (BB-1), *Massachusetts* (BB-2), *Iowa* (BB-4), *Wisconsin* (BB-9), and *Illinois* (BB-7). NH 42525

1st Commanding Officer: Capt. F. Rodgers

Authorized: June 30, 1890

Keel Laid: June 25, 1891

Launched: June 10, 1893

Commissioned: June 10, 1896

Sponsor: Miss Leila Herbert

Displacement Standard Tons: 10,288

Design Crew Complement: 32 officers, 441 enlisted

Main Guns: 4-13" 35 caliber, 8-8" 35 caliber, 4-6" 40 caliber

Secondary Guns: 20-6 pounder, 6-1 pounder

Construction Costs: $4 maximum plus armament

Armor: Maximum thickness 18" at turret face plates

Length Overall: 350'11"

Mean Draught: 24' maximum 28'

Extreme Beam: 69'3"

Torpedo Tubes: 6-18" surface

Catapults: None

Builder: William Cramp & Sons, Philadelphia

Original Engines Manufactured: Cramp type: vertical inverted triple expansion 3 cylinder reciprocating

Original Boilers Manufactured: Cramp type: FT; no. 6

Original Fuel: Coal 1640 tons

Drive: Reciprocating 2 screws

Sisters: *Indiana* class

Designed Speed: 15 knots

Designed Shaft Horsepower: 9000

Design Comments: Sea-going coast-line Battleship

History Highlights:
- March 27, 1898 "Flying Squadron" for blockade of Cuba
- May 22, 1898 with bombardment of Santiago de Cuba
- Missed July 3, 1898 Battle of Santiago de Cuba, while at Guantanamo Bay for coaling
- 1898–1905 with Atlantic Squadron decommissioned Jan. 8, 1906
- Reduced commission May 2, 1910
- Recommissioned June 9, 1917 as gunnery training ship
- Assigned to battle practice "A" Battleship Forces June 6, 1918–June 9, 1919

Date Decommissioned: March 31, 1919; stricken Nov. 22, 1919

Commendations: None

Final Disposition: Scuttled off Pensacola Bar, Florida, on Jan. 1, 1921; Feb. 20, 1925 returned to Navy; Nov. 15, 1956 declared property of the state of Florida

Massachusetts, photographed on Sept. 5, 1899. NH 73767

1st Commanding Officer: Capt. H. L. Howison
Authorized: June 30, 1890
Keel Laid: Nov. 19, 1891
Launched: Oct. 26, 1893
Commissioned: July 15, 1896
Sponsor: Miss Daisy Ainsworth
Displacement Standard Tons: 11,688
Design Crew Complement: 32 officers, 441 enlisted
Main Guns: 4-13" 35 caliber, 8-8" 35 caliber, 4-6" 40 caliber
Secondary Guns: 20-6pounder 6-1 pounder
Construction Costs: $4 million max plus armament
Armor: Maximum thickness 18" at turret face plates
Length Overall: 351'2"
Mean Draught: 24', maximum 28'
Extreme Beam: 69'3"
Torpedo Tubes: 6-18" surface
Catapults: None
Builder: Union Iron Works, San Francisco
Original Engines Manufactured: Union Iron Works, vertical inverted triple expansion 3 cylinder reciprocating
Original Boilers Manufactured: Union Iron Works, type: FT; no. 6
Original Fuel: Coal, 1640 tons
Drive: Reciprocating 2 screws
Sisters: *Indiana* class
Designed Speed: 16 knots
Designed Shaft Horsepower: 9000

Oregon, photographed in her original configuration. NH 44467

Design Comments: Sea-going coast-line Battleship
History Highlights:
- 1896 to Pacific Fleet; March 12, 1898–May 24, 1898 from San Francisco to Florida on record 74-day cruise
- July 3, 1898 Battle of Santiago de Cuba, Spanish-American War; October, 1898 to Asiatic Squadron
- June 28, 1900 grounded on rocks in the straits of Pechili in Pacific off China during the Boxer Rebellion
- Grounding repairs at Kure, Japan; to Asia 1903–1906
- Decommissioned at Puget Sound on April 4, 1906; recommissioned August 29, 1911 in/out of reserve on West Coast
- April 17, 1917 WWI commission as escort for Siberian expedition to Russia
- Decommissioned June 12, 1919 at Bremerton; recommission August 21–Oct. 4, 1919 for fleet review at Seattle by President Wilson
- Jan. 4, 1924 in accordance with Washington Naval Treat; rendered incapable of war service

Date Decommissioned: In June, 1925, loaned to the state of Oregon as a memorial; Feb. 17, 1941 reclassified as IX-22; towed to Guam July, 1944
Commendations: None
Final Disposition: March 15, 1956 sold for scrap to Massey Co; sold to Iwai Sanggo Co., towed to Kawasaki, Japan, and scrapped

Oregon, (IX-22, ex-BB-03) being scrapped at Kawasaki, Japan, in September, 1956. NH 3007

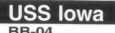

Iowa, under fire by battleship guns of *Mississippi* (BB-41), while in the last phase of her target service, off Panama on March 22, 1923. *Iowa* sank as a result of this shelling. NH 96027

1st Commanding Officer: Capt. W. T. Sampson
Authorized: July 19, 1892
Keel Laid: August 5, 1893
Launched: March 28, 1896
Commissioned: June 16, 1897
Sponsor: Miss M. L. Drake
Displacement Standard Tons: 11,410
Displacement Full Load Tons:
Design Crew Complement: 36 officers, 450 enlisted
Main Guns: 4-12" I 35 caliber, 8-8" 35 caliber, 6-4" 40 caliber
Secondary Guns: 20-6 pounder, 4-1 pounder, 4-.30 caliber
Construction Costs: $4 million maximum plus armament
Armor: Maximum thickness 15" at turret face plates
Length Overall: 362'5"
Mean Draught: 24', 28' maximum
Extreme Beam: 72'3"
Torpedo Tubes: 4-14" surface
Catapults: None
Builder: William Cramp & Sons, Philadelphia
Original Engines Manufactured: Cramp type: vertical inverted triple expansion 3 cylinder reciprocating
Original Boilers Manufactured: Cramp type: FT; no. 5
Original Fuel: Coal, 1795 tons
Drive: Reciprocating, 2 screws
Sisters: *Iowa* Class

Designed Speed: 16 knots
Designed Shaft Horsepower: 11,000
Design Comments: Sea-going coast-line Battleship
History Highlights:
- July 3, 1898 Battle of Santiago de Cuba, damaged the Spanish cruisers *Marie Teresa*, *Oquendo*, *Viscaya* was beached
- Also damaged the destroyers *Pluton* and *Furor* during the Battle of Santiago
- Oct. 12, 1898 to Pacific Fleet; February 1902 to Flagship South Atlantic Squadron; Dec. 23, 1903 decommissioned at New York
- Dec. 23, 1903 recommissioned to North Atlantic Squadron; June 30, 1905 in the John Paul Jones commemoration
- July 6, 1907 in reserve; decommissioned at Philadelphia; July 23, 1908 recommissioned May 2, 1910 as a training ship and Atlantic Reserve Fleet
- May 27, 1914 decommissioned at Philadelphia; April 23, 1917 in limited commission as a receiving ship and trainer
- WWI served as training ship and provided guard duty at entrance to the Chesapeake Bay
- April 30, 1919 as coast BB-4, was first radio-controlled target ship in fleet exercises

Date Decommissioned: March 31, 1919
Commendations: none
Final Disposition: March 23, 1923 sunk with 14" shells by *Mississippi* (BB-41) in Panama Bay

Iowa, running trials prior to her commissioning in 1897. Note Cramp Shipbuilding Co. House flag.

USS Kearsarge
BB-05

1st Commanding Officer: Capt. W. M. Folger

Authorized: March 2, 1895

Keel Laid: June 30, 1896

Launched: March 24, 1898

Commissioned: February 20, 1900

Sponsor: Mrs. Herbert Winslow

Displacement Standard Tons: 11,540

Displacement Full Load Tons: 12,320

Design Crew Complement: 40 officers, 514 enlisted, Flagship 586

Main Guns: 4-13" 35 caliber, 4-8" 35 caliber, 14-5" 40 caliber

Secondary Guns: 20-6 pounder, 8-1 pounder, 4-.30 caliber

Construction Costs: $4 million maximum plus armament

Armor: maximum thickness 17" at turret face plates

Length Overall: 375'4"

Mean Draught: 23'6"

Extreme Beam: 72'3"

Torpedo Tubes: 4-18" surface

Catapults: None

Builder: Newport News Ship Building Co., Newport News, Virginia

Original Engines Manufactured: Newport News type: vertical inverted triple expansion 3 cylinder reciprocating

Original Boilers Manufactured: Newport News type: FT; no. 5

Original Fuel: Coal, 1591 tons

Drive: Reciprocating 2 screws

Sisters: *Kearsarge* Class

Designed Speed: 16 knots

Designed Shaft Horsepower: 10,000

Design Comments: Sea-Going coast-line Battleship
- Named by Act of Congress to commemorate famed steam sloop of the Civil War

History Highlights:
- Flagship, North Atlantic Squadron 1903; Flagship June 3–July 26, 1903 European Squadron; Dec. 10, 1903 to formal opening Guantanamo Bay, Cuba
- April 13, 1906 off Cape Cruz, Cuba—an accident with a 13" gun killed 2 officers and 8 enlisted men
- Dec. 16, 1907–Feb. 22, 1909 sailed with the Great White Fleet; September 4, 1909–June 23, 1915 decommissioned at Philadelphia for modernization
- Feb. 4, 1916 at Philadelphia Atlantic Reserve Fleet, WWI East Coast; August 18, 1918 rescued survivors of the vessel *Nordhav* sunk by U 117
- May 29, 1919–August 29, 1919 last cruise as a Battleship; decommissioned May 10, 1920 at Philadelphia and converted to crane ship AB-1 on August 5, 1920
- As AB-1 crane ship with a 250-ton lift capability raised the sunken submarine *Squalus*
- Nov. 6, 1941 designated *Crane Ship* 1 to give name to aircraft carrier *Kearsarge* (CV-12), later to CV-33
- Fit guns on Battleships *Indiana, Alabama, Pennsylvania,* and cruisers *Savannah* and *Chicago*

Date Decommissioned
- May 10, 1920 as Battleship
- Nov. 6, 1941 as AB-1
- June 22, 1955 as *Crane Ship*-1

Commendations: None

Final Disposition: Struck from the Navy list on June 22, 1955; sold for scrapping on August 9, 1955

14 Crane Ship-1 (AB-1) ex-K*earsarge*, lifting 250-ton load during tests at Philadelphia Navy Yard on Oct. 27, 1922, a career that would last until 1955. NH 52038

Kearsarge, photo taken prior to 1909 and installation of cage masts. NH 61238

USS Kentucky

BB-06

Kentucky, photo taken early in her career prior to the installation of cage masts. NH 67839

1st Commanding Officer: Capt. C. H. Chester
Authorized: March 2, 1985
Keel Laid: June 30, 1896
Launched: March 24, 1898
Commissioned: May 15, 1900
Sponsor: Miss Christine Bradley
Displacement Standard Tons: 11,540
Displacement Full Load Tons: 12,320
Design Crew Complement: 40 officers, 514 enlisted, Flagship 586
Main Guns: 4-13" 35 caliber, 4-8" 35 caliber, 12-5" 40 caliber
Secondary Guns: 20-6 pounder, 8-1 pounder, 4-.30 caliber
Construction Costs: $4 million maximum plus armament
Armor: Maximum thickness 17" at turret face plates
Length Overall: 375'4"
Mean Draught: 23'6"
Extreme Beam: 72'3"
Torpedo Tubes: 4-18" surface
Catapults: None
Builder: Newport News Ship Building Co., Newport News, Virginia
Original Engines Manufactured: Newport News type: vertical inverted triple expansion 3 cylinder reciprocating
Original Boilers Manufactured: Newport News type FT; no. 5
Original Fuel: Coal, 1591 tons
Drive: Reciprocating 2 screws
Sisters: *Kearsarge* class

Designed Speed: 16 knots
Designed Shaft Horsepower: 10,000
Design Comments: Sea-going coast-line Battleship
History Highlights:
- To Asiatic Station at Manila on Feb. 3, 1901; Flagship Southern Squadron March 23, 1901; to New York May 23, 1904
- Oct. 1, 1906 at Havana to protect U.S. interests; at Norfolk on April 15, 1907 for the Jamestown Exposition
- Sailed with Great White Fleet of Dec. 16, 1907 to Feb. 22, 1909
- Decommissioned August 28, 1909 at Norfolk; recommissioned June 4, 1912 2nd Reserve—in ordinary at Philadelphia May 31, 1913
- Recommissioned June 23, 1915; off Mexico to protect American interests June 2, 1916
- WWI as training ship in Chesapeake Bay and Atlantic Coast to Long Island Sound
- Last cruise with midshipmen May 29, 1919 to August 27, 1919
- To Philadelphia Navy Yard August 30, 1919
Date Decommissioned: May 29, 1920
Commendations: None
Final Disposition: Sold to Dravo Construction Co. Jan. 23, 1924 for scrapping in accordance with Washington Naval Treaty of Feb. 8, 1922

USS Illinois
BB-07

1st Commanding Officer: Capt. G. A. Converse
Authorized: June 10, 1896
Keel Laid: Feb. 10, 1897
Launched: Oct. 4, 1898
Commissioned: Sept. 16, 1901
Sponsor: Miss Nancy Leiter
Displacement Standard Tons: 11,565
Displacement Full Load Tons: 12,150
Design Crew Complement: 40 officers, 496 enlisted
Main Guns: 4-13" 35 caliber, 14-6" 40 caliber
Secondary Guns: 16-6 pounder. 6-1 pounder, 4-.30 caliber
Construction Costs: $3.75 million maximum plus armament
Armor: Maximum thickness 16.5" at turret face plates
Length Overall: 375'4"
Mean Draught: 23'6"
Extreme Beam: 72'3"
Torpedo Tubes: 4-18" surface
Catapults: None
Builder: Newport News Ship Building Co., Newport News, Virginia
Original Engines Manufactured: Newport News type: vertical triple expansion 3 cylinder reciprocating
Original Boilers Manufactured: Newport News type: FT; no. 8
Original Fuel: Coal, 1400 tons
Drive: Reciprocating, 2 screws
Sisters: *Illinois* Class
Designed Speed: 16 knots

Designed Shaft Horsepower: 10,000
Design Comments: Sea-going coast-line Battleship
History Highlights:
- December 1901 Algiers, Louisiana to test drydock; May 1902 to European Squadron
- July 14, 1902 grounded in harbor at Christiana, Norway; repair at Chatham, England in September, 1902
- January, 1903, with *Connecticut* and *Culgoa*, to Messina, Italy for earthquake relief
- Sailed with Great White Fleet, Dec. 16, 1907 to Feb. 22, 1909
- August 4, 1909 at Boston, decommissioned; April 15, 1912 reserve commission; Nov. 2, 1912 recommissioned
- 1919 at Philadelphia Navy Yard; Oct. 23, 1921 loaned to State of New York for naval militia
- Washington Naval Treaty ship made not fit for war service duty; fitted as a floating armory to New York in 1924
- Reclassified IX-15 on Jan. 8, 1941 to use name for *Illinois* (BB-65); IX-15 as *Prairie State* for State of New York until Dec. 31, 1955

Date Decommissioned: 1924 as BB-07, WWII as U.S. Naval Reserve in New York
Commendations: None
Final Disposition: May 18, 1956 towed to Baltimore, Maryland and sold for scrapping to Bethlehem Steel Co.

Illinois, photo taken early in her career, while she still had her military masts. NH 73783

1st Commanding Officer: Capt. W. H. Brownson
Authorized: June 10, 1896
Keel Laid: Dec. 2, 1896
Launched: May 18, 1898
Commissioned: Oct. 16, 1900
Sponsor: Miss Mary Morgan
Displacement Standard Tons: 11,565
Displacement Full Load Tons: 12,150
Design Crew Complement: 40 officers, 496 enlisted
Main Guns: 4-13" 35 caliber, 14-6" 40 caliber
Secondary Guns: 16-6 pounder, 6-1 pounder, 4-.30 caliber
Construction Costs: $3.75 million maximum plus armament
Armor: Maximum thickness 16.5" at turret face plates
Length Overall: 374'
Mean Draught: 23'6"
Extreme Beam: 72'3"
Torpedo Tubes: 4-18" surface
Catapults: None
Builder: William Cramp & Sons, Philadelphia
Original Engines Manufactured: Cramp type: vertical inverted triple expansion 3 cylinder reciprocating
Original Boilers Manufactured: Cramp type: FT; no. 8
Original Fuel: Coal, 1355 tons
Drive: Reciprocating, 2 screws

Sisters: *Illinois* Class
Designed Speed: 16 knots
Designed Shaft Horsepower: 10,000
Design Comments: Sea-going coast-line Battleship
History Highlights:
- 1900 to North Atlantic Station; May 4–August 4 Mediterranean cruise; Feb. 11–16, 1907 pacification duty in Cuba
- Sailed with Great White Fleet of Dec. 16, 1970 to Feb. 22, 1909
- Arrived at New York with BB-10 *Maine*, Oct. 20, 1908 in advance of Great White Fleet
- In reserve at New York Nov. 3, 1908; August 17, 1909–July 1, 1912 out of commission at New York
- July 1, 1912 recommission with Atlantic Fleet; Oct. 31, 1913 in ordinary at Philadelphia; July 1, 1914 in reserve as training vessel
- Recommissioned April 5, 1917 as Flagship of Division 1 Battleship Force; Atlantic Fleet WWI as training ship

Date Decommissioned: May 7, 1920 and transferred to War Dept on Sept.15, 1921 for use as a target ship
Commendations: None
Final Disposition: Used as a target ship during bombing tests Sept. 27, 1921; hulk sold for scrap on March 19, 1924

Alabama, photographed about 1908, probably off San Diego, California. Note that she still had her two military masts. NH 73315

ALABAMA AFTER COMPLETION
OF BOMBING

A PORT SIDE VIEW

SHOWING THE FOREMAST AND STACKS

A HOLE IN THE STARBOARD SIDE
FORWARD

A CLOSE UP OF THE STACKS

HOLE IN STARBOARD SIDE AFT

Alabama, a sequence of photos showing her after use as a target in experiments in aircraft bombing on Sept. 27, 1921, Chesapeake Bay, Maryland. NH 57493

USS Wisconsin
BB-09

1st Commanding Officer: Capt. G. C. Reiter
Authorized: June 10, 1896
Keel Laid: Feb. 9, 1897
Launched: Nov. 26, 1898
Commissioned: Feb. 4, 1901
Sponsor: Miss Elizabeth Stephenson
Displacement Standard Tons: 11,653
Displacement Full Load Tons: 12,150
Design Crew Complement: 35 officer, 496 enlisted
Main Guns: 4-13" 35 caliber, 14-6" 40 caliber
Secondary Guns: 16-6 pounder, 6-1 pounder, 4-.30 caliber
Construction Costs: $3.75 million maximum plus armament
Armor: Maximum thickness 16.5" at turret face plates
Length Overall: 373'10"
Mean Draught: 23'8"
Extreme Beam: 72'3"
Torpedo Tubes: 4-18" surface
Catapults: None
Builder: Union Iron Works, San Francisco
Original Engines Manufactured: Union Iron Works type: vertical inverted triple expansion 3 cylinder reciprocating
Original Boilers Manufactured: Union Iron Works type: FT; no. 8
Original Fuel: Coal, 1310 tons
Drive: Reciprocating 2 screws
Sisters: *Illinois* Class
Designed Speed: 16 knots

Designed Shaft Horsepower: 10,000
Design Comments: Sea-going coast-line Battleship
History Highlights:
- 1901 to Pacific Fleet; 1901 and 1902 Pacific Cruise; 1902 Flagship, Pacific Squadron
- May 13, 1903 to Asiatic Station; 1903–1906 Flagship Asiatic Squadron; Nov. 15, 1906 decommissioned; April 1, 1908 recommissioned
- Sailed with Great White Fleet of Dec. 16 1907 to Feb. 22, 1909
- June, 1909 to Atlantic Fleet; January to March 1910 Atlantic cruise; April 1910 in reserve at Portsmouth, New Hampshire
- April, 1912 to Philadelphia with Reserve Atlantic Fleet. October, 1913 in ordinary. July, 1915 to the Naval Academy Practice Squadron
- April 23, 1918 WWI to Coastal Battleship Patrol Squadron as Engineering School ship
- June 19, 1918 midshipmen cruise in York River, 1918 and 1919 Atlantic cruise and midshipmen cruise

Date Decommissioned: Decommissioned at Philadelphia May 20, 1920; classified as BB-9 on July 17, 1920
Commendations: None
Final Disposition: Sold for scrap on Jan. 26, 1922 in accordance with Washington Naval Treaty of Feb. 8, 1922

Wisconsin, photographed early in her career with two military masts. NH 61956

Maine, photo taken early in her career with two military masts. NH 74103

1st Commanding Officer: Capt. E. H. C. Leutze

Authorized: May 4, 1898

Keel Laid: Feb. 15, 1899

Launched: July 27, 1901

Commissioned: Dec. 29, 1902 at Philadelphia

Sponsor: Miss Mary Preble Anderson

Displacement Standard Tons: 12,846

Displacement Full Load Tons: 13,500

Design Crew Complement: 40 officers, 521 enlisted

Main Guns: 4-12" 45 caliber, 16-6" 50 caliber

Secondary Guns: 6-3" 50 caliber; 8-3 pounder; 6-1 pounder 3-.30 caliber

Construction Costs: $3 million maximum plus armor and armament

Armor: Maximum thickness 12" at turret face plates

Length Overall: 393' 11"

Mean Draught: 24'4"

Extreme Beam: 72'3"

Torpedo Tubes: 2-18" submerged

Catapults: None

Builder: William Cramp & Sons, Philadelphia

Original Engines Manufactured: Cramp type, vertical inverted triple expansion 3 cylinder reciprocating

Original Boilers Manufactured: Nicalusse type: WT; no. 4

Original Fuel: Coal, 1867 tons

Drive: Reciprocating, 2 screws

Sisters: *Maine* Class

Designed Speed: 18 knots

Designed Shaft Horsepower: 16,000

Design Comments:

· Sea-going, coast-line battleship

History Highlights:

• 1903–1907 cruised alng the Atlantic Coast to the West Indies

• Dec. 16, 1907 to October, 1908 part of the "Great White Fleet" joining at San Francisco, California

· 1908 fitted as Flagship of 3rd Squadron, Atlantic Fleet; decommissioned at Portsmouth, New Hampshire on August 31, 1909

• During WWI used for training engineers, armed guard crews and midshipmen

• Part of "Review of the Fleet," New York, Dec. 26, 1918

• Operated with the Atlantic Fleet until May 15, 1920; classified as BB-10 on July 17, 1920

Date Decommissioned: May 15, 1920 sold to J. G. Hitner and W. F. Cutler of Philadelphia

Commedations: None

Final Disposition: Made incapable of war on Dec. 17, 1923; scrapped in accordance with the Washington Naval Treaty of Feb. 8, 1922

1st Commanding Officer: Capt. W. S. Cowles

Authorized: May 4, 1898

Keel Laid: Feb. 7, 1900

Launched: Dec. 28, 1901

Commissioned: Dec. 1, 1903

Sponsor: Mrs. Edson Galludet

Displacement Standard Tons: 12,362

Displacement Full Load Tons: 13,500

Design Crew Complement: 40 officers, 521 enlisted

Main Guns: 4-12" 45 caliber, 16-6" 50 caliber

Secondary Guns: 6-3" 50, 8-3 pounder 6-1 pounder, 2-.30 caliber

Construction Costs: $3 million maximum plus armor and armament

Armor: Maximum thickness 12" at turret face plates

Length Overall: 393'11"

Mean Draught: 23'9"

Extreme Beam: 72'3"

Torpedo Tubes: 2-18" submerged

Catapults: None

Builder: Newport News Ship Building Co., Newport News, Virginia

Original Engines Manufactured: Newport News type: vertical inverted triple expansion 4 cylinder reciprocating

Original Boilers Manufactured: Thornycraft Newport News type: WT; no. 24

Original Fuel: Coal, 1837 tons

Drive: Reciprocating 2 screws

Sisters: *Maine* Class

Designed Speed: 18 knots

Designed Shaft Horsepower: 16,000

Design Comments: Sea-going coast-line Battleship

History Highlights:

- April 13, 1904 flareback in port gun, aft turret, set off powder charges, killing 36 crewmen
- Sailed with the Great White Fleet of Dec. 16, 1907 to Feb. 22, 1909
- June 9, 1905 to Mediterranean; Jan 17–19, 1907 earthquake relief to Kingston, Jamaica
- April 1907 Jamestown Exposition; May 1, 1910 in reserve; June 1, 1911 to Atlantic Fleet; decommissioned at Philadelphia on March 16, 1914
- In ordinary at Philadelphia on Dec. 2, 1914; recommissioned on April 15, 1915; reserve fleet at Philadelphia on Oct. 18, 1915; recommissioned on May 2, 1916; in ordinary December, 1916
- Recommissioned April 23, 1917 for WWI, Atlantic Fleet at Yorktown, Virginia, training ship at Chesapeake Bay
- Division 2 Atlantic Fleet training for engineering and gunnery
- Feb. 18–Sept. 19, 1919 to and from Brest, France, returning troops from Europe

Date Decommissioned: Sept. 8, 1919 at Philadelphia; sold to J. G. Hitner and W. F. Cutler of Philadelphia on Jan. 26, 1922

Final Disposition: Scrapped in accordance with the Washington Naval Treaty of Feb. 8, 1922

Missouri, photo taken early in her career with two military masts. NH 61216

USS Ohio
BB-12

1st Commanding Officer: Capt. L. C. Logan
Authorized: May 4, 1898
Keel Laid: April 22, 1899
Launched: May 18, 1901
Commissioned: Oct. 4, 1904
Sponsor: Miss Helen Deschler
Displacement Standard Tons: 12,723
Displacement Full Load Tons: 13,500
Design Crew Complement: 40 officers, 521 enlisted
Main Guns: 4-12" 45 caliber, 16-6" 50 caliber
Secondary Guns: 6-3" 50 caliber, 8-3" pounder, 6-1
    pounder, 2-.30 caliber
Construction Costs: $3 million maximum plus armor
    and armament
Armor: Maximum thickness 12" at turret face plates
Length Overall: 393'10"
Mean Draught: 23'10"
Extreme Beam: 72'3"
Torpedo Tubes: 2-18" submerged
Catapults: None
Builder: Union Iron Works, San Francisco
Original Engines Manufactured: Union Iron Works type: vertical
    inverted triple expansion 3 cylinder reciprocating
Original Boilers Manufactured: Thornycraft Union Iron
    Works type: WT; no. 12
Original Fuel: Coal, 2150 tons
Drive: Reciprocating 2 screws
Sisters: *Maine* Class
Designed Speed: 18 knots
Designed Shaft Horsepower: 16,000
Design Comments: Sea-going coast-line Battleship
History Highlights:
· April 1, 1905 far East tour of inspection to Japan, China
    and the Philippines with Secretary of War William
    H. Taft

Ohio, on trials in San Francisco Bay, July 26, 1904 NH 63139

· Sailed with Great White Fleet of Dec. 16, 1907 to Feb.
    22, 1909
· 1909 to Atlantic Fleet and New York Naval militia
· April 1914 to Vera Cruz, Mexico; 1915 to reserve fleet at
    Philadelphia
1915 and 1916 recommissioned for midshipmen summer
    cruises
· April 24, 1917 recommissioned for WWI training gun
    crews and engineers
· To Philadelphia on Nov. 28, 1918, placed in reserve on
    Jan. 7, 1919
Date Decommissioned: At Philadelphia on May 31, 1922
Commendations: None
Final Disposition: Sold for scrap on March 24, 1923

"Great White Fleet" transits the Suez Canal,
January, 1909. Battleships of the fleet nearing
Port Said, circa January 5–6, 1909.
Ohio (BB-12) is at right. NH 101494

USS Virginia
BB-13

1st Commanding Officer: Capt. S. Schroeder

Authorized: March 3, 1899

Keel Laid: May 21, 1902

Launched: April 5, 1904

Commissioned: May 7, 1906

Sponsor: Miss Gay Montague

Displacement Standard Tons: 14,948

Displacement Full Load Tons: 16,094

Design Crew Complement: 40 officers, 772 enlisted

Main Guns: 4-12" 40 caliber. 8-18" 45 caliber. 12-6" 50 caliber

Secondary Guns: 12-3" 50 caliber, 12-3 pounder, 8-.30 caliber

Construction Costs: $3.6 million maximum plus armor and armament

Armor: Maximum thickness 12" at turret face places

Length Overall: 441'3"

Mean Draught: 23'9"

Extreme Beam: 76'3"

Torpedo Tubes: 4-21" submerged

Catapults: None

Builder: Newport News Ship Building Co., Newport News, Virginia

Original Engines Manufactured: Newport News type: vertical inverted triple expansion 4 cylinder reciprocating

Original Boilers Manufactured: Newport News Niclausse type: WT; no. 12

Original Fuel: Coal, 1900 tons

Drive: Reciprocating 2 screws

Sisters: *Virginia* Class

Designed Speed: 19 knots

Designed Shaft Horsepower: 19,000

Design Comments: Sea-going coast-line Battleship

History Highlights:

· April 9, 1906 shakedown along East Coast; September–October at Havana, Cuba to protect American interests

· April, 1907 Hampton Roads for Jamestown Tricentennial

· Sailed with Great White Fleet of Dec. 16, 1907 to Feb. 22, 1909

· November to December, 1909 European cruise; 1910–1913 with Atlantic Fleet; April 14, 1914 off Vera Cruz, Mexico

· March 20, 1916 in reserve at Boston; WWI gunnery training ship out of Port Jefferson and Norfolk

· December, 1917 temporary Flagship Battleship Division 1; December, 1917 temporary Flagship Battleship Division 3; 1918 convoy duty

· December, 1918–July, 1919 troop transport duty to and from Brest, France

· 1919 at Boston

Date Decommissioned: Decommissioned August 13, 1920 and struck from Navy list, for sale; to War Department on August 6, 1923 for target ship

Commendations: None

Final Disposition: With *New Jersey* (BB-16) to Diamond Shoals, Cape Hatteras, North Carolina; sunk as a target ship on Sept. 5, 1923

Virginia, photographed circa 1907, about a year after commissioning and before the installation of cage masts, dressed with flags and with rails manned. NH 96128

Virginia, sinks after use as a bombing target off Diamond Shoals, Cape Hatteras, North Carolina, on Sept. 5, 1923 by General Billy Mitchell's Air Corps.   NATIONAL ARCHIVES PHOTO 19-N-12633

USS Nebraska
BB-14

1st Commanding Officer: Capt. R. F. Nicholson
Authorized: March 3, 1899
Keel Laid: July 4, 1902
Launched: Oct. 7, 1904
Commissioned: July 1, 1907
Sponsor: Miss Mary N. Mickey
Displacement Standard Tons: 14,948
Displacement Full Load Tons: 16,094
Design Crew Complement: 40 officers, 772 enlisted
Main Guns: 4-12" 40 caliber, 8-8" 45 caliber, 12-6" 50 caliber
Secondary Guns: 12-3" 50 caliber, 12-3 pounder, 8-.30 caliber
Construction Costs: $3.6 million maximum plus armor and armament
Armor: Maximum thickness 12" at turret face plates
Length Overall: 441'3"
Mean Draught: 23'9"
Extreme Beam: 76'3"
Torpedo Tubes: 4-21" submerged
Catapults: None
Builder: Moran Brothers, Seattle, Washington
Original Engines Manufactured: Moran type: vertical inverted triple expansion 4 cylinder reciprocating
Original Boilers Manufactured: Moran, Babcock and Wilcox type: WT; no. 12
Original Fuel: Coal, 1700 tons
Drive: Reciprocating, 2 screws
Sisters: *Virginia* Class
Designed Speed: 19 knots
Designed Shaft Horsepower: 19,000
Design Comments: Sea-going coast-line Battleship; was originally named *Pennsylvania*

History Highlights:
- After shakedown and alterations joined Great White Fleet at San Francisco, replacing *Alabama* (BB-08)
- With Atlantic Fleet at Hudson-Fulton celebration in 1910; to Hampton Roads on Feb. 22, 1912
- Mexican service at Vera Cruz, May 1–June 21, 1914, Oct. 13, 1916; reduced commission, full commission on April 3, 1917
- WWI April 6, 1917 at Boston Naval Yard; Chesapeake Bay and East Coast to April 15, 1918
- May 16, 1918 returned body of Uruguay's minister to his home country; returned to Hampton Roads on July 26, 1918
- Convoy duty Sept. 17, 1918–Dec. 2, 1918; troop transport duty Dec. 30, 1918–June 21, 1919
- June 22, 1919 to Division 2 Squadron 1, Pacific Fleet
- Operated on the West Coast under the command of Capt. P. N. Olmstead until decommissioned on July 2, 1920

Date Decommissioned: July 2, 1920 possibly at San Francisco; classified BB-14 on July 17, 1920
Commendations: None
Final Disposition: Rendered incapable of war service on Nov. 9, 1923; scrapped in accordance with Washington Naval Treaty of Feb. 8, 1922

Nebraska, photographed in 1908, approximately a year after commissioning. NH 63137

Nebraska, at the Norfolk Navy Yard, Portsmouth, Virginia on April 20, 1918, about eight months before the end of World War I. Note the camouflage designed to make range-finding more difficult. NH 60235

Georgia, photographed in 1907, during her first year of service. NH 73911

1st Commanding Officer: Capt. R. Davenport

Authorized: March 3, 1899

Keel Laid: August 31, 1901

Launched: Oct. 11, 1904

Commissioned: Sept. 24, 1906 at Boston

Sponsor: Miss Stella Tate

Displacement Standard Tons: 14,948

Displacement Full Load Tons: 16,094

Design Crew Complement: 40 officers, 772 enlisted

Main Guns: 4-12" 40 caliber, 8-8" 45 caliber, 12-6" 50 caliber

Secondary Guns: 12-3" 50 caliber, 12-3 pounder, 8-.30 caliber

Construction Costs: $3.6 million maximum plus armor and armament

Armor: Maximum thickness 12" at turret face plates

Length Overall: 441"3"

Mean Draught: 23'9"

Extreme Beam: 76'3"

Torpedo Tubes: 4-21 submerged

Catapults: None

Builder: Bath Iron Works, Bath, Maine

Original Engines Manufactured: Bath type: vertical inverted triple expansion 4 cylinder reciprocating

Original Boilers Manufactured: Bath, Niclausse type: WT; no. 12

Original Fuel: Coal, 1925 tons

Drive: Reciprocating, 2 screws

Sisters: *Virginia* Class

Designed Speed: 19 knots

Designed Shaft Horsepower: 19,000

Design Comments: Sea-going coast-line Battleship

History Highlights:

· October 1906 at Atlantic Fleet Division 2, Squadron 1; April, 1907 Jamestown Exposition

· July 15, 1907 powder charge ignited, killing 10, in aft 8" turret

· Sailed with the Great White Fleet of Dec. 16, 1907 to Feb. 22, 1909

· 1909 to Dec. 20, 1915 Atlantic Fleet, also in Cuban and Mexican waters at periods of civil unrest

· Jan. 27, 1916 decommissioned at Boston; recommissioned for WWI 3rd Division Battleship Force

· Dec. 10, 1918–June, 1919 troop transport force to and from Brest, France

· July 16, 1919 to Pacific Fleet at San Diego and to Mare Island for repairs

Date Decommissioned: July 15, 1920

Commendations: None

Final Disposition: Sold for scrap on Nov. 1, 1923; name struck from the Navy list on Nov. 10, 1923

USS New Jersey
BB-16

1st Commanding Officer: Capt. W. W. Kimball
Authorized: June 7, 1900
Keel Laid: April 2, 1902
Launched: Nov. 10, 1904
Commissioned: May 12, 1906
Sponsor: Mrs. William B. Kennedy
Displacement Standard Tons: 14,948
Displacement Full Load Tons: 16,094
Design Crew Complement: 40 officers, 772 enlisted
Main Guns: 4-12" 40 caliber, 8-8" 45 caliber, 12-6" 50 caliber
Secondary Guns: 12-3" 50, 12-3 pounder, 2-1 pounder, 6-.30 caliber
Construction Costs: $3.6 million maximum plus armor and armament
Armor: Maximum thickness 12" at turret face plates
Length Overall: 441'3"
Mean Draught: 23'9"
Extreme Beam: 76'3"
Torpedo Tubes: 4-21" submerged
Catapults: None
Builder: Fore River Co., Quincy, Massachusetts
Original Engines Manufactured: Fore River type: vertical inverted triple expansion 4 cylinder reciprocating
Original Boilers Manufactured: Fore River, Babcock & Wilcox type: WT; no. 12

Original Fuel: Coal, 1955 tons
Drive: Reciprocating 2 screws
Sisters: *Virginia* Class
Designed Speed: 19 knots
Designed Shaft Horsepower: 19,000
Design Comments: Sea-going Battleship
History Highlights:
· Review by President Theodore Roosevelt in Oyster Bay, September 1906; Sept. 21–Oct. 13, 1906 at Havana, Cuba, to protect American interests
· Sailed with Great White Fleet of Dec. 16, 1907 to Feb. 22, 1909
· Great White Fleet commanded by Rear Admiral Robley D. Evans and Rear Admiral Charles S. Sperry
· May 2, 1910–July 15, 1911 out of commission in reserve at Boston
· 1912 and 1913 midshipmen cruises; April, 1914 off Vera Cruz, Mexico, to protect American interests
· WWI training gunner and seamen recruits in Chesapeake Bay
· Troop transport after WWI armistice to and from Brest until June 9, 1919
Date Decommissioned: At Boston Naval Yard August 6, 1920
Commendations: None
Final Disposition: Sunk off Cape Hatteras, North Carolina on Sept. 5, 1923 by Gen. B. Mitchell; bomb tests along with *Virginia* (BB-13)

New Jersey, firing her forward turrets, during short-range gunnery practice, circa 1913. Note that she had cage masts in place of her earlier military masts. NH 101062

USS Rhode Island
BB-17

1st Commanding Officer: Capt. P. Garst
Authorized: June 7, 1900
Keel Laid: May 1, 1902
Launched: May 17, 1904
Commissioned: Feb. 19, 1906
Sponsor: Mrs. F. C. Dumaine
Displacement Standard Tons: 14,948
Displacement Full Load Tons: 16,094
Design Crew Complement: 40 officers, 772 enlisted
Main Guns: 4-12" 40 caliber, 8-8" 45 caliber, 12-6" 50 caliber
Secondary Guns: 12-3" 50 caliber, 12-3 pounder, 2-1 pounder, 6-.30 caliber

Rhode Island, photographed on July 8, 1909 at the New York Navy Yard with one cage mast and one military mast. NH 44368

Construction Costs: $3.6 million maximum plus armor and armament
Armor: Maximum thickness 12" at turret face plates
Length Overall: 441'3"
Mean Draught: 23'9"
Extreme Beam: 76'3"
Torpedo Tubes: 4-21" submerged
Catapults: None
Builder: Fore River Shipbuilding Co., Quincy, Massachusetts
Original Engines Manufactured: Fore River type: vertical inverted triple expansion 4 cylinder reciprocating
Original Boilers Manufactured: Fore River Babcock & Wilcox type: WT; no. 12
Original Fuel: Coal, 1700 tons
Drive: Reciprocating, 2 screws
Sisters: *Virginia* Class
Designed Speed: 19 knots
Designed Shaft Horsepower: 19,000
Design Comments: Sea-going Battleship; extensive shake-down and acceptance test between Boston and Hampton Roads
History Highlights:
- Division 2, Squadron 1 Atlantic Fleet Jan. 1, 1907; Dec. 8, 1907 Hampton Roads; review of Great White Fleet before it sailed
- Sailed with Great White Fleet f Dec. 16, 1907 to Feb. 22, 1909
- March 8, 1909 Division 3, Squadron 1 Atlantic Fleet; Flagship, Division 3, Squadron 1 July 17, 1912; Vera Cruz, Mexico from November, 1913 to February, 1914
- Flagship, Division 4, Squadron 1 December, 1914 to January 1915; reduced commission in reserve at Boston May 15, 1916
- Flagship C.I.C. Reserve Force Atlantic Fleet June 24, 1916 to Sept. 28, 1916; full commission at Hampton Roads March 27, 1917
- Flagship; Commander Battleship Division 3 Atlantic Fleet May 3, 1917; WWI Gunnery practice and drills
- Troop transport duty to and from Brest, France from December, 1918 to July 1919
- Flagship Battleship Squadron 1, Pacific Fleet July 17, 1919 at Mare Island, California into 1920
Date Decommissioned: June 30, 1920, placed in reserve fleet
Commendations: None
Final Disposition: Rendered incapable of warlike service Oct. 4, 1923; scrapped on Nov. 1, 1923

USS Connecticut
BB-18

1st Commanding Officer: Capt. W. Swift
Authorized: July 1, 1902
Keel Laid: March 10, 1903
Launched: Sept. 29, 1904
Commissioned: Sept. 29, 1906
Sponsor: Miss A. Welles
Displacement Standard Tons: 16,000
Displacement Full Load Tons: 17,650
Design Crew Complement: 42 officers, 785 enlisted, Flagship 916
Main Guns: 2-12" 45 caliber, 12-8" 45 caliber, 12-7" 45 caliber
Secondary Guns: 20-3" 50 caliber, 12-3 pounder 4-1 pounder 4-.030 caliber
Construction Costs: $4.212 million maximum plus armor and armament
Armor: Maximum thickness 12" at turret face plates
Length Overall: 456'4"
Mean Draught: 24'6"
Extreme Beam: 76'10"
Torpedo Tubes: 4-21 submerged
Catapults: None
Builder: New York Navy Yard, Brooklyn, N.Y.
Original Engines Manufactured: New York Navy Yard type: vertical triple expansion 4 cylinders reciprocating
Original Boilers Manufactured: Babcock & Wilcox type: WT; no. 12
Original Fuel: Coal, 2249 tons
Drive: Reciprocating 2 screws
Sisters: *Connecticut* Class

Designed Speed: 18 knots
Designed Shaft Horsepower: 16,500
Design Comments: First-class Battleship
History Highlights:
- Flagship, Atlantic Fleet April 16, 1907; April, 1907 Presidential fleet review and opening ceremonies of the Jamestown Exposition
- Great White Fleet as Flagship; Atlantic Fleet and Flagship fleet from Dec. 16, 1907 to Feb. 22, 1909
- Flagship of Atlantic Fleet to 1912; Nov. 2, 1910 to March 17, 1911 European cruise on scouting problems
- 1913–1915 4th Division Atlantic Fleet usually as Flagship; Oct. 3, 1916 Flagship, 5th Division Battleship force, Atlantic
- WWI based in York River, Virginia; exercised in Chesapeake Bay training midshipmen and gun crews
- Troop transport duty Jan. 6, 1919 to June 22, 1919 to and from Brest, France
- June 23, 1919 Flagship Battleship Squadron 2 Atlantic Fleet; 1920 midshipmen cruise Caribbean; 1921 midshipmen cruise to Europe
- August 21, 1921 Flagship training, Pacific Fleet; 1922 cruise, Pacific coast to Puget Sound Dec. 16, 1922
- To Puget Sound Dec. 16, 1922; decommissioned March 1, 1923 at Puget Sound

Date Decommissioned: To Puget Sound Dec. 16, 1922, decommissioned March 1, 1923 at Puget Sound
Commendations: None
Final Disposition: Sold for scrap Nov. 1, 1923 in accordance with the Washington Naval Treaty of Feb. 8, 1922

Connecticut prior to her conversion to cage masts.
NH 61553

USS Lousisiana
BB-19

1st Commanding Officer: Capt. A. R. Couden
Authorized: July 1, 1902
Keel Laid: Feb. 7, 1903
Launched: August 27, 1904
Commissioned: June 2, 1906
Sponsor: Miss Juanita LaLande
Displacement Standard Tons: 16,000
Displacement Full Load Tons: 17,650
Design Crew Complement: 42 officers, 785 enlisted, Flagship 916
Main Guns: 4-12" 45 caliber, 12-8" 45 caliber 12-7" 45 caliber
Secondary Guns: 20 3" 50 caliber, 12-3 pounder, 2-1 pounder
Construction Costs: $4.212 million maximum plus armor and armament
Armor: Maximum thickness 12" at turret face plates
Length Overall: 456'4"
Mean Draught: 24'6"
Extreme Beam: 76'10"
Torpedo Tubes: 4-21 submerged
Catapults: None
Builder: Newport News Shipbuilding Co., Newport News, Virginia
Original Engines Manufactured: Newport News type: vertical 4 cylinder triple expansion reciprocating
Original Boilers Manufactured: Babcock & Wilcox type; WT; no. 12

Original Fuel: Coal, 2376 tons
Drive: Reciprocating 2 screws
Sisters: *Connecticut* Class
Designed Speed: 18 knots
Designed Shaft Horsepower: 16,500
Design Comments: First-class Battleship
History Highlights:
- Sept. 15, 1906 to Havana with William H. Taft and Robert Bacon on Peace Commission
- Nov. 8, 1906 with President Theodore Roosevelt to Panama for inspection of work on the Canal
- Sailed with the Great White Fleet of Dec. 16, 1907 to Feb. 22, 1909
- Nov. 1, 1910 joined 2nd Division of the Atlantic Fleet
- July 6, 1913 to Sept. 24, 1915, time spent in Mexican waters protecting American property and supporting the Monroe Doctrine
- 1915 to WWI in reserve at Norfolk, Virginia; served as training ship for midshipmen
- WWI gunnery and engineering training ship; Sept. 25, 1918 escort duty to Halifax, Nova Scotia
- Dec. 24, 1918 troop transport duty to and from Brest, France

Date Decommissioned: Oct. 20, 1920 decommissioned at Philadelphia Navy Yard
Commendations: None
Final Disposition: Nov. 1, 1923 sold for scrap

Louisiana underway sometime between 1910 and 1914, after conversion to cage masts.
NH 51421

. . . .

Vermont, photographed about 1907 before conversion to cage masts. NH 63580

1st Commanding Officer: Capt. W. P. Potter

Authorized: March 3, 1903

Keel Laid: May 21, 1904

Launched: August 31, 1905

Commissioned: March 4, 1907 at Boston

Sponsor: Miss Jennie Bell

Displacement Standard Tons: 16,000

Displacement Full Load Tons: 17,650

Design Crew Complement: 42 officers, 838 enlisted, Flagship 916

Main Guns: 4-12" 45 caliber, 12-8" 45 caliber, 12-7" 45 caliber

Secondary Guns: 20-3" 50 caliber, 10-3 pounder. 2-1 pounder, 6-.030 caliber

Construction Costs: $4.212 million maximum plus armor and armament

Armor: Maximum thickness 12" at turret face plates

Length Overall: 456'4"

Mean Draught: 24'6"

Extreme Beam: 76'10"

Torpedo Tubes: 4-21" submerged

Catapults: None

Builder: Fore River Shipbuilding Co. Quincy, Massachusetts

Original Engines Manufactured: Fore River type: vertical 4 cylinder triple expansion reciprocating

Original Boilers Manufactured: Babcock & Wilcox type: WT; no. 12

Original Fuel: Coal, 2405 tons

Drive: Reciprocating 2 screws

Sisters: *Vermont* Class

Designed Speed: 18 knots

Designed Shaft Horsepower: 16,500

Design Comments: First-class Battleship

History Highlights:

· 1907 shakedown and to Atlantic Fleet, Division 1

· Sailed with Great White Fleet of Dec. 16, 1907 to Feb. 22, 1909

· 1910–1917 with Atlantic Fleet; April 15, 1914 off Vera Cruz, Mexico

· August 26, 1917 to Nov. 4, 1918 as an engineering training ship in the Chesapeake Bay area

· Jan. 9, 1919–June 20, 1919 as a troop transport ship to and from Europe

· Inactivated as battleship at Philadelphia in 1919; to Mare Island, California on Sept. 18, 1919

· Classified as BB-20 on July 17, 1920

Date Decommissioned: June 30, 1920 inactive at Mare Island until Nov. 10, 1923

Commendations: None

Final Disposition: Struck Nov. 11, 1923; sold for scrap on Nov. 30, 1923 in accordance with the Washington Naval Treaty of Feb. 8, 1922

1st Commanding Officer: Capt. C. E. Vreeland

Authorized: March 3, 1903

Keel Laid: Feb. 10, 1904

Launched: August 12, 1905

Commissioned: April 18, 1907 at Philadelphia

Sponsor: Miss Anna Hoch

Displacement Standard Tons: 16,000

Displacement Full Load Tons: 17,650

Design Crew Complement: 42 officers, 838 enlisted, Flagship 916

Main Guns: 4-12" 45 caliber, 12-8" 45 caliber, 12-7" 45 caliber

Secondary Guns: 20-3" 50 caliber, 12-3 pounder, 2-1 pounder, 2-.030 caliber

Construction Costs: $4.212 million maximum plus armor and armament

Armor: Maximum thickness 12" at turret face plates

Length Overall: 456'4"

Mean Draught: 24'6"

Extreme Beam: 76'10"

Torpedo Tubes: 4-21 submerged

Catapults: None

Builder: New York Shipbuilding Corporation, Camden, New Jersey

Original Engines Manufactured: New York Shipbuilding type: vertical 4 cylinder triple expansion reciprocating

Original Boilers Manufactured: Babcock & Wilcox type: WT; no. 12

Original Fuel: Coal, 2310 tons

Drive: Reciprocating, 2 screws

Sisters: *Vermont* class

Designed Speed: 18 knots

Designed Shaft Horsepower: 16,500

Design Comments: First-class Battleship

History Highlights:

- Sailed with Great White Fleet of Dec. 16, 1907 to Feb. 22, 1909
- 1910 Atlantic Fleet 2nd Battleship Division; midshipmen cruise 1912; 1913 cruise to Italy
- April 6, 1917 at Philadelphia Navy Yard at outbreak of WWI; to New York and the 4th Battleship Division
- Served in WWI as an engineering training ship in Chesapeake Bay area
- After Armistice performed transport duty to and from Brest, France
- 1920 to Pacific and Honolulu, Seattle, San Francisco and San Pedro, California
- 1920 Flagship Battleship Division 4, Squadron 2, for Rear Admiral Hughes; 1920 to Pacific area and return 1921
- From June 1921 to September 1921 to Norway, Portugal, Gibraltar and Guantanamo Bay

Date Decommissioned: Dec. 16, 1921 at Philadelphia Navy Yard

Commendations: None

Final Disposition: Stricken on August 24, 1923, sold for scrap in accordance with Washington Naval Treaty of Feb. 8, 1922

Kansas, photo taken while on trial runs 1906, prior to her commissioning on April 18, 1907.
NH 61136

1st Commanding Officer: Capt. J. Hubbard

Authorized: March 3, 1903

Keel Laid: Oct. 27, 1903

Launched: April 8, 1905

Commissioned: March 9, 1907

Sponsor: Miss Rose Marie Schaller

Displacement Standard Tons: 16,000

Displacement Full Load Tons: 17,650

Design Crew Complement: 42 officers, 838 enlisted, Flagship 916

Main Guns: 4-12" 45 caliber, 12-8" 45 caliber, 12-7" 45 caliber

Secondary Guns: 20-3" 50 caliber, 12-3 pounder, 2-1 pounder, 2-.030 caliber

Construction Costs: $4.212 maximum plus armor and armament

Armor: Maximum thickness 12" at turret face plates

Length Overall: 456'4"

Mean Draught: 24'6"

Extreme Beam: 76'10"

Torpedo Tubes: 4-21" submerged

Catapults: None

Builder: Newport News Shipbuilding Co., Newport News, Virginia

Original Engines Manufactured: Newport News type: vertical 4 cylinder triple expansion reciprocating

Original Boilers Manufactured: Babcock & Wilcox type: WT; no. 12

Original Fuel: Coal, 2387 tons

Drive: Reciprocating, 2 screws

Sisters: *Vermont* Class

Designed Speed: 18 knots

Designed Shaft Horsepower: 16,500

Design Comments: First-class Battleship

History Highlights:

· Sailed with the Great White Fleet of Dec. 16, 1907 to Feb. 22, 1909

· April 6, 1917 date U.S. entered WWI; joined active fleet at Tangier Sound

· Division 4 Battleship force as a gunnery and engineering training ship

· Sept. 29, 1918 at 38,11' N latitude; 74,41' W longitude; damage to starboard side by a mine laid by U-117

· March 11, 1919 cruiser and transport service to July 23, 1919

· July, 1919 to November 1921 used as a training ship

· Midshipmen summer cruises 1920 and 1921

Date Decommissioned: Dec. 1, 1921, stricken Dec. on 1, 1921

Commendations: None

Final Disposition: Dismantled and scrapped by the Philadelphia Navy Yard on Jan. 23, 1924

Minnesota, photographed in 1911, probably near Hampton, Virginia. Note the fire control gear on the No. 1 turret.
NH 73978

1st Commanding Officer: Capt. J. Fremont

Authorized: March 3, 1903

Keel Laid: May 12, 1904

Launched: Sept. 30, 1905

Commissioned: Feb. 1, 1908 at Philadelphia

Sponsor: Miss M. C. Money

Displacement Standard Tons: 13,000

Displacement Full Load Tons: 14,465

Design Crew Complement: 34 officers, 710 enlisted

Main Guns: 4-12" 45 caliber, 8-8" 45 caliber, 8-7" 45 caliber

Secondary Guns: 12-3" 50 caliber, 6-3 pounder, 2-1 pounder, 6-.030 caliber

Construction Costs: $3.5 million plus armor and armament

Armor: Maximum thickness 12" at turret face plates

Length Overall: 382'

Mean Draught: 24'8"

Extreme Beam: 77'

Torpedo Tubes: 2-21" submerged

Catapults: None

Builder: William Cramp & Sons, Philadelphia

Original Engines Manufactured: Cramp type: vertical 4-cylinder triple expansion reciprocating

Original Boilers Manufactured: Babcock & Wilcox type: WT; no. 8

Original Fuel: Coal, 1800 tons

Drive: Reciprocating, 2 screws

Sisters: *Mississippi* Class

Designed Speed: 17 knots

Designed Shaft Horsepower: 10,000

Design Comments: First-class Battleship

History Highlights:

- 1908–1909 Atlantic Fleet; Feb. 10, 1910 joined the Great White Fleet on its return to port
- May 1, 1910 to June 7, 1910 Mississippi River cruise to namesake state
- June 19, 1912 to el Cuero Cuba to protect American interests
- August 1, 1912 in first reserve; Dec. 30, 1913 as aeronautic station ship at Pensacola, Florida
- April 21, 1913 to Vera Cruz, Mexico to protect American interests and act as a base for aviators at Vera Cruz
- July 10, 1914 at Newport News to prepare for transfer to Greek Navy after being sold to Greece
- July 21, 1914 decommissioned and turned over to the Greek Navy; renamed *Lemnos*

Date Decommissioned: Newport News July 21, 1914

Commendations: None

Final Disposition: Served in the Greek Navy as a coastal defense vessel; sunk in Salamis Harbor on April, 1941 by German aircraft; scrapped after World War II

Mississippi, in a photo taken around 1908, possibly during her first year of active service. NH 50123

Greek coastal defence ship *Lemnos*, ex-M*ississippi* (BB-23), at the naval base of Salamis near Athens, Greece as seen from a German Heinkel HE 60 seaplane after the occupation of the base by the German army in April, 1941. NH 54430

1st Commanding Officer: Capt. S. W. B. Diehl

Authorized: March 3, 1903

Keel Laid: May 12, 1904

Launched: Dec. 9, 1905

Commissioned: April 1, 1908 at Philadelphia

Sponsor: Miss Louise Gooding

Displacement Standard Tons: 13,000

Displacement Full Load Tons: 14,465

Design Crew Complement: 34 officers, 710 enlisted

Main Guns: 4-12" 45 caliber; 8-8" 45 caliber; 8-7" 45 caliber

Secondary Guns: 12-3" 50 caliber; 6-3 pounder, 2-1 pounder; 5-.030 caliber

Construction Costs: $3.5 million maximum plus armor and armament

Armor: Maximum thickness 12" at turret face plates

Length Overall: 382'

Mean Draught: 24'8"

Extreme Beam: 77'

Torpedo Tubes: 2-21" submerged

Catapults: None

Builder: William Cramp & Sons, Philadelphia

Original Engines Manufactured: Cramp type; vertical 4-culinder triple expansion reciprocating

Original Boilers Manufactured: Babcock & Wilcox type: WT; no. 8

Original Fuel: Coal, 1800 tons

Drive: Reciprocating, 2 screws

Sisters: *Mississippi* Class

Designed Speed: 17 knots

Designed Shaft Horsepower: 10,000

Design Comments: First-class battleship

History Highlights:

- Atlantic Fleet 1908; at Hampton Roads for review of the return on Feb. 22, 1909 of the "Great White Fleet"
- Oct. 20, 1909 to British and French waters for exercises
- May 4, 1911 for cruise up the Mississippi to Louisiana ports
- Oct. 27, 1913 in reserve at Philadelphia; May 9, 1914 to the Mediterranean for midshipmen
- July 17, 1914 at Villefrache, Greece for transfer to the Greek navy after being sold to Greece
- Decommissioned July 30, 1914 and transferred to Greece as *Kilkis*

Date Decommissioned: July 30, 1914 at Villefroche, Greece

Commendations: None

Final Disposition: Sunk in Salamis Harbor by German aircraft in April, 1941; scrapped after WWII

Idaho at the Naval Review in October of 1912. NH 60505

Greek coastal defence ship *Lemnos*, ex-*Mississippi* (BB-23), and Greek coastal defence ship *Kilkis*—the ex-*Idaho* (BB-24). Sunk in the basin of the Greek naval base of Salamis after aerial attacks of the Luftwaffe, as seen from the pier of the harbor by the advancing German army in April, 1941. NH 77440

New Hampshire in the Hudson River, New York, on Dec. 27, 1918. (Last American pre-dreadnought.) NH 2891

1st Commanding Officer: Capt. C. M. Winslow
Authorized: April 27, 1904
Keel Laid: May 1, 1905
Launched: June 30, 1906
Commissioned: March 19, 1908
Sponsor: Miss Hazel E. McLane
Displacement Standard Tons: 16,000
Displacement Full Load Tons: 17,650
Design Crew Complement: 41 officers, 809 enlisted
Main Guns: 4-12" 45 caliber, 8-8" 45 caliber, 8-7" 45 caliber
Secondary Guns: 20-3" 50 caliber, 2-1 pounder, 2-0.30 caliber
Construction Costs: $4.4 million plus armor and armament
Armor: Maximum thickness 12" at turret face plates
Length Overall: 456'4"
Mean Draught: 24'6"
Extreme Beam: 76'10"
Torpedo Tubes: 4-21 submerged
Catapults: None
Builder: New York Shipbuilding Corporation, Camden, New Jersey
Original Engines Manufactured: New York Shipbuilding type: vertical 4 cylinder triple expansion reciprocating
Original Boilers Manufactured: Babcock & Wilcox type: WT; no. 12
Original Fuel: Coal, 2287 tons
Drive: Reciprocating, 2 screws
Sisters: *Vermont* Class

Designed Speed: 18 knots
Designed Shaft Horsepower: 16,500
Design Comments: First-class Battleship
History Highlights:
- With U.S. Marine expeditionary force to Panama from June 20 to June 26, 1908
- Participated in the Naval Review welcoming home the Great White Fleet at Hampton Roads
- 1909 to Atlantic Fleet; 1910 Battleship Division 2, cruise to England, and France, then to Germany and Russia
- 1912 and 1913 midshipmen cruises; off Hispaniola in December of 1912; off Vera Cruz, Mexico on April 15, 1914
- December, 1916 at Santo Domingo, where her captain took part in the government
- Spent WWI training gunners and engineers; convoy duty Sept. 15 to Dec. 24, 1918
- Troop transport from Dec. 24, 1918 to June 22, 1919; overhauled at Philadelphia from June, 1919 to June, 1920; Flagship special mission to Haiti on October, 1920 to January, 1921
- Jan. 25, 1921 Swedish minister to home till March 24, 1921; return to Philadelphia
Date Decommissioned: May 21, 1921 at Philadelphia Navy Yard
Commendations: None
Final Disposition: Sold for scrapping on Nov. 1, 1923, in accordance with the Washington Naval Treaty of Feb. 8, 1922.

USS South Carolina
BB-26

1st Commanding Officer: Capt. A. F. Fechteler

Authorized: March 3, 1905

Keel Laid: Dec. 18, 1906

Launched: July 1, 1908

Commissioned: March 1, 1910

Sponsor: Miss Frederica Ansel

Displacement Standard Tons: 16,000

Displacement Full Load Tons: 17,617

Design Crew Complement: 51 officers, 818 enlisted, 1354 for war service

Main Guns: 8-12" 45 caliber (15,000-yard range with armor-piercing rounds)

Secondary Guns: 23-2" 50 caliber; 4-1 pounder 2-.030 caliber

Construction Costs: $4.4 million plus armor and armament

Armor: Maximum thickness 12" at turret face plates

Length Overall: 452'9"

Mean Draught: 24'6"

Extreme Beam: 80'3"

Torpedo Tubes: 2-21" submerged

Catapults: None

Builder: William Cramp & Sons, Philadelphia

Original Engines Manufactured: Cramp type: vertical 4 cylinder triple expansion reciprocating

Original Boilers Manufactured: Babcock & Wilcox type: WT; no. 12

Original Fuel: Coal, 2380 tons

Drive: Reciprocating, 2 screws

Sisters: *South Carolina* Class

Designed Speed: 18.5 knots

Designed Shaft Horsepower: 16,500

Design Comments: First American single caliber Battleship class

History Highlights:

· March 6, 1910 shakedown cruise; June 17–18, 1910 at New York for reception for Theodore Roosevelt

· November, 1910 with Battleship Division 2; 1911 Naval Review at New York; May 28, 1913 at New York City *Maine* Memorial Commemoration

· September, 1910 to January, 1912 "Big Stick" to the Gulf of Mexico and the Caribbean; September, 1913 at Vera Cruz, Mexico

· Jan. 28, 1914 landed U.S. Marines at Port-au-Prince, Haiti

· WWI U-boat duty and commerce raider duty along the U.S. East Coast

· Sept. 9, 1918 convoy duty to the Middle Atlantic

· February–July, 1919 troop transport duty to and from Brest, France; June 5, 1920 to September, 1920 Pacific cruise with midshipmen

· Atlantic cruise in 1921 with midshipmen

Date Decommissioned: Dec. 15, 1921 at Philadelphia Navy Yard

Commendations: None

Final Disposition: Struck from the Navy list on Nov. 10, 1923; scrapped on April 24, 1924 in accordance with the Washington Naval Treaty of Feb. 8, 1922

South Carolina, photographed on March 5, 1910, four days after commissioning. (First American dreadnought.) NH 44251

USS Michigan
BB-27

1st Commanding Officer: Capt. N. R. Rusher

Authorized: March 3, 1905

Keel Laid: Dec. 17, 1906

Launched: May 26, 1908

Commissioned: Jan. 4, 1910

Sponsor: Mrs. F. W. Brooks

Displacement Standard Tons: 16,000

Displacement Full Load Tons: 17,617

Design Crew Complement: 51 officers, 818 enlisted, 1354 for war service

Main Guns: 8-12" 45 caliber (15,000-yard range with armor-piercing rounds)

Secondary Guns: 23-3" 50 caliber; 4-1 pounder 2-.030 caliber

Construction Costs: $4.4 million plus armor and armament

Armor: Maximum thickness 12" at turret face plates

Length Overall: 452'9"

Mean Draught: 24'6"

Extreme Beam: 80'3"

Torpedo Tubes: 2-21"submerged

Catapults: None

Builder: New York Shipbuilding Corporation, Camden, New Jersey

Original Engines Manufactured: New York Shipbuilding type; vertical 4 cylinder triple expansion reciprocating

Original Boilers Manufactured: Babcock & Wilcox type: WT; no. 12

Original Fuel: Coal, 2380 tons

Drive: Reciprocating, 2 screws

Sisters: *South Carolina* Class

Designed Speed: 18.5 knots

Designed Shaft Horsepower: 16,500

Michigan, photographed taken circa 1916–17. NH 86376

Design Comments: First American single caliber Battleship class

History Highlights:
- January, 1919 assigned to the Atlantic Fleet; July 6, 1912 in the Gulf of Mexico to protect American interests in Mexico
- April 16, 1914 off Vera Cruz, Mexico to protect American interests and honor
- Oct. 21, 1914 WWI off the Atlantic Coast; April 6, 1917 assigned to Battleship Force 2 for escort convoy and training
- December, 1918 to April 26, 1919 transport duty returning troops to the U.S. from Europe
- August 6, 1919 limited commission at Philadelphia Navy Yard, then reactivated
- Various sailings and cruises 1919–1922
- Final cruise from Hampton Roads to Philadelphia Navy Yard August 31, 1921 to Sept. 1, 1921

Date Decommissioned: Feb. 11, 1922 decommissioned at Philadelphia; stricken Nov. 10, 1923 in accordance with the Washington Naval Treaty

Commendations: None

Final Disposition: She and four other Battleships scrapped at the Philadelphia Naval Yard during 1924

Michigan, being scrapped at the Philadelphia Navy Yard, Jan. 5, 1925. NH 60650

USS Delaware
BB-28

1st Commanding Officer: Capt. C. A. Gove

Authorized: June 29, 1906

Keel Laid: Nov. 11, 1907

Launched: Feb. 6, 1909

Commissioned: April 4, 1910

Sponsor: Mrs. A. P. Cahall

Displacement Standard Tons: 20,380

Displacement Full Load Tons: 22,000

Design Crew Complement: 55 officers, 878 enlisted, 1384 for war service

Main Guns: 10-12" 45 caliber (15,000-yard range with armor-piercing rounds)

Secondary Guns: 14-5" 50 caliber

Construction Costs: $6 million maximum plus armor and armament

Armor: Maximum thickness 12" at turret face plates

Length Overall: 518'9"

Mean Draught: 27'4"

Extreme Beam: 85'3"

Torpedo Tubes: 2-21" submerged

Catapults: None

Builder: Newport News Shipbuilding Co., Newport News, Virginia

Original Engines Manufactured: Newport News type: vertical 4 cylinder triple expansion reciprocating

Original Boilers Manufactured: Babcock & Wilcox type: WT; no. 14

Original Fuel: Coal, 2668 tons

Drive: Reciprocating, 2 screws

Sisters: *Delaware* Class

Designed Speed: 21 knots

Designed Shaft Horsepower: 25,000

Design Comments: First-class Battleship

History Highlights:

- Oct. 3–Oct. 10 at Wilmington, Delaware; Nov 1, 1910 cruise to England and France with First Division, Atlantic Fleet
- June 19–28, 1911 at Portsmouth, England; Fleet review by King George V; Fleet exercises from 1912 to 1917
- Naval Review with President Taft Oct. 14, 1912; France cruise with *Utah* (BB-31) and *Wyoming* (BB-32) in 1913
- 1914 and 1915 off Vera Cruz, Mexico during political and civil disturbances
- Nov. 25, 1917 with U.S. Battleship Division 9 to Scapa Flow to join 6th Battle Squadron of the British Grand Fleet
- Feb. 8, 1918 off Stavanger, Norway; attacked by German submarine and evaded 2 torpedoes
- March and April, 1918 convoy duty with Grand Fleet; June 30 to July 2, 1918 cruise with 6th Battle Squadron; returned to the U.S. on August 12, 1918
- Atlantic Fleet cruises and midshipmen summer cruises 1918–1923

Date Decommissioned: Norfolk Navy Yard crew transferred to *Colorado* (BB-45); decommissioned on Nov. 10, 1923

Commendations: None

Final Disposition: Stripped of war capability; sold for scrapping on Feb. 5, 1924 in accordance with the Washington Naval Treaty of Feb. 8, 1922

Above: *Delaware* during the Naval Review in October, 1912.
NH 60575

Below: The World War I "Fleet" returning from target practice in Cuban waters on April 15, 1919. *Delaware* (BB-28) follows the other battleships into New York Harbor. NH 63331

North Dakota running trials in 1909. NH 44731

1st Commanding Officer: CDR. C. P. Plunkett

Authorized: March 2, 1907

Keel Laid: Dec. 16, 1907

Launched: Nov. 10, 1908

Commissioned: April 11, 1910 at Boston

Sponsor: Miss Mary Benton

Displacement Standard Tons: 20,000

Displacement Full Load Tons: 22,000

Design Crew Complement: 55 officers, 878 enlisted, 1384 for war service

Main Guns: 10-12" 45 caliber (15,000-yard range with armor-piercing rounds)

Secondary Guns: 14-5" 50 caliber

Construction Costs: $6 million maximum plus armor and armament

Armor: Maximum thickness 12" at turret face plates

Length Overall: 510' waterline, 518'9" overall

Mean Draught: 26'11"

Extreme Beam: 85'3"

Torpedo Tubes: 2-21" submerged

Catapults: None

Builder: Fore River Co., Quincy, Massachusetts

Original Engines Manufactured: Curtis (Fore River) type cruising turbine

Original Boilers Manufactured: Babcock & Wilcox type: WT; no. 14

Original Fuel: Coal, 2676 tons and oil, 380 tons

Drive: Turbine Drive, 4 screws

Sisters: *Delaware* Class

Designed Speed: 21 knots

Designed Shaft Horsepower: 25,000

Design Comments: First-class Battleship; coal- and oil-fired boilers

History Highlights:

· 1910 to the Atlantic Fleet; Nov. 2, 1910 to England and France for a visit

· Summer of 1912 and 1913 midshipmen cruises

· April 26, 1914 off Vera Cruz, Mexico; Atlantic Fleet prepared for WWI with more training

· Was in Chesapeake Bay at the outbreak of WWI; spent WWI training gunners and engineers

· Nov. 13, 1919 out of Norfolk to carry remains of the Italian ambassador back to Italy

· Summer of 1921 took part in Army-Navy bomb tests off Virginia Capes

· German warships *Frankfurt* and *Ostfriesland* were sunk by Gen. Billy Mitchell

· To 1923 Fleet exercises and midshipmen summer cruises

Date Decommissioned: Nov. 22, 1923 at Norfolk Navy Yard

Commendations: None

Final Disposition: Struck from the Navy list on Jan. 7, 1931; sold for scrapping on March 16, 1931

USS Florida
BB-30

1st Commanding Officer: Capt. H. S. Knapp
Authorized: May 13, 1908
Keel Laid: March 9, 1909
Launched: May 12, 1910
Commissioned: Sept. 15, 1911
Sponsor: Miss E. D. Fleming
Displacement Standard Tons: 21,825
Displacement Full Load Tons: 23,033
Design Crew Complement: 60 officers, 941 enlisted, 1422 for war service
Main Guns: 10-12" 45 caliber (15,000-yard range with armor-piercing rounds)
Secondary Guns: 16-5" 51 caliber
Construction Costs: $6 million maximum plus armament
Armor: Maximum thickness 12" at turret face plates
Length Overall: 510' waterline, 521'6"
Mean Draught: 28'4"
Extreme Beam: 88'3"
Torpedo Tubes: 2-21" submerged
Catapults: None
Builder: New York Navy Yard, Brooklyn, N.Y.
Original Engines Manufactured: New York Navy Yard, Parsons type; turbine
Original Boilers Manufactured: Babcock & Wilcox type; WT; no. 12
Original Fuel: Coal, 2500 tons and oil, 400 tons
Drive: Turbine drive, 4 screws
Sisters: *Florida* Class

Designed Speed: 20.75 knots
Designed Shaft Horsepower: 28,000
Design Comments: First-class Battleship, coal- and oil-fired boilers
History Highlights:
- November, 1911 to March, 1912 shakedown off Maine and in the Caribbean; March 29, 1912 Flagship Atlantic Fleet Division 1
- 1912–1914 Normal Fleet operations; February 1914 to Vera Cruz, Mexico; October, 1914 to Atlantic Fleet Division 2
- Dec. 7, 1917 with Battleship Division 9 to join the 6th Battle Squadron, British Grand Fleet WWI
- Present at the surrender of German High Seas Fleet at Scapa Flow on Nov. 21, 1918
- Escort ship for liner *George Washington* carrying President Wilson to Brest, France on Dec. 12 and 13, 1918
- Victory naval review in North River at New York City late in December, 1918
- Jan. 4, 1919 to Norfolk and normal peacetime operations
- 1920–1931 Atlantic Fleet operations, cruise with marines in Caribbean, midshipmen training cruises
Date Decommissioned: at Philadelphia on Feb. 16, 1931
Commendations: None
Final Disposition: Scrapped in accordance with the London Naval Treaty of 1930

Above: Battleship Division Five, Atlantic Fleet. Three of the division's ships steaming in line abreast, during an exercise, circa 1921. Ships are (front to back): *Florida* (BB-30), *Delaware* (BB-28), *North Dakota* (BB-29). NH 93421

Below: *Florida* off New York City on Oct. 3, 1911, during the Naval Review. NH 61261

1st Commanding Officer: Capt. W. S. Benson

Authorized: May 13, 1908

Keel Laid: March 15, 1909

Launched: Dec. 23, 1909

Commissioned: August 31, 1911 at Philadelphia

Sponsor: Miss Mary Alice Spry

Displacement Standard Tons: 21,825

Displacement Full Load Tons: 23,033

Design Crew Complement: 60 officers, 941 enlisted, 1422 for war service

Main Guns: 10-12" 45 caliber (15,000-yard range with armor-piercing rounds)

Secondary Guns: 16-5" 51 caliber

Construction Costs: $6 million maximum plus armor and armament

Armor: Maximum thickness 12" at turret face plates

Length Overall: 510' waterline, 521'6" overall

Mean Draught: 28'4"

Extreme Beam: 88'3"

Torpedo Tubes: 2-21 submerged

Catapults: None

Builder: New York Shipbuilding Corporation, Camden, New Jersey

Original Engines Manufactured: New York Shipbuilding Parsons type; turbine

Original Boilers Manufactured: Babcock & Wilcox type: WT; no. 12

Original Fuel: Coal, 2520 tons and oil, 400 tons

Drive: Turbine drive, 4 screws

Sisters: *Florida* Class

Utah on Oct. 3, 1911 at the Fleet Review. Note the torpedo boat off her bow. NH 63200

Utah (AG-16, ex-BB-31) photo taken circa 1939 possibly before or after Puget Sound refit.

NH 83596

Utah (AG-16) photo of memorial plaque on the ship's wreck at Pearl Harbor on Dec. 9, 1950.

NATIONAL ARCHIVES PHOTOGRAPH 80-G-484354

Designed Speed: 21 knots

Designed Shaft Horsepower: 28,000

Design Comments: First-class Battleship, coal- and oil-fired boilers

History Highlights:

- September, 1911 to March, 1912 shakedown cruises; March 12 with the Atlantic Fleet; April 21, 1914 landed U.S. Marines at Vera Cruz, Mexico
- WWI with Battleship Division 6 and returned to the U.S. on Dec. 25, 1918; classified BB-31 on July 17, 1920; Oct. 21, 1920 with Battleship Division 5
- October, 1925 to December, 1925 modernized at Norfolk; 1926 to 1931 with the Atlantic Fleet
- July 1, 1931 changed from BB-31 to AG-16 (Mobile Target Ship) converted at Norfolk; recommissioned April 1, 1932
- April–June, 1932 shakedown; to the Pacific Fleet on June 30, 1932; 1932 to 1941 as mobile radio-controlled target ship

- 1935 fitted and used as a machine gun training ship; May–September, 1941 overhauled at Puget Sound
- Was berthed at F 11 Battleship Row at Pearl Harbor on Dec. 7, 1941; at 0812 hours she rolled over and sank from a torpedo hit
- Dec. 29, 1941 declared "in ordinary"; Sept. 5, 1944 out of commission, not in service; partially sunk hull is still at Pearl Harbor with an unknown number of men still entombed inside

Date Decommissioned: Converted to AG-16 as part of compliance to the London Navy Treaty of April 22, 1930

Commendations: One Battle Star for WWII as the AG-16

Final Disposition: Stricken on Nov. 13, 1944; *Utah* Memorial at Pearl Harbor; ship's bells are on display in Salt Lake City and Clearfield, Utah

USS Wyoming
BB-32

1st Commanding Officer: Capt. F. L. Chapin

Authorized: March 3, 1909

Keel Laid: Feb. 9, 1910

Launched: May 25, 1911

Commissioned: Sept. 25, 1912 at Philadelphia

Sponsor: Miss Dorothy Eunice Knight

Displacement Standard Tons: 26,000

Displacement Full Load Tons: 27,243

Design Crew Complement: 58 officers, 1005 enlisted, 1594 for war service, 1663 for Flagship

Main Guns: 12-12" 50 caliber (16,000-yard range with armor-piercing rounds)

Secondary Guns: 21-5" 51 caliber

Construction Costs: $6 million maximum plus armor and armament

Armor: Maximum thickness 12" at turret face plates

Length Overall: 554' waterline, 562' overall

Mean Draught: 28'6"

Extreme Beam: 93'3"

Torpedo Tubes: 2-21" submerged

Catapults: None

Builder: William Cramp & Sons, Philadelphia

Original Engines Manufactured: Cramp , Parsons type: turbine

Original Boilers Manufactured: Babcock & Wilcox type; no. 12

Original Fuel: Coal 2641, tons, and oil, 400 tons

Drive: Turbine drive, 4 screws

Sisters: *Wyoming* Class

Designed Speed: 21 knots

Designed Shaft Horsepower: 28,000

Design Comments: First-class Battleship; coal- and oil-fired boilers

History Highlights:

- 1912 to Atlantic Fleet; Flagship Atlantic Fleet; 1912 midshipmen cruise; fall, 1912, European cruise
- 1914–1915 Fleet drills; April, 1914 off Vera Cruz, Mexico; Nov. 25, 1917 with Battleship Division 9; to 6th Battleship Squadron of British Grand Fleet; present at the surrender of the German High Seas Fleet at Scapa Flow on Nov. 21, 1918
- Feb. 6, 1918 dodged torpedo off Stavanger, Norway
- Jan. 13, 1919 Flagship, Battleship Division 7, 3rd Squadron; July 1, 1919 Flagship Battleship Division 6 Squadron 4 Pacific Fleet; 1919–1921 Pacific Fleet drill
- August 19, 1921 Flagship Atlantic Fleet until 1927; Sept. 9, 1930 Flagship Commander Training Squadron, Scout Fleet; Jan. 1, 1931 converted to a training ship (AG-17)
- 1931–1936 Atlantic Fleet training; Jan. 5, 1937 to Pacific; April, 1937 to Atlantic Fleet; June 31, 1937 to Keil, Germany
- 1937–1941 training ship for Naval Reserve and Merchant Marine
- 1942–1946 provided training as "Chesapeake Raider" of the Operational Training Command

Date Decommissioned: July 11, 1947 to Norfolk; August 1, 1947 decommissioned as AG-17

Commendations: None

Final Disposition: Struck from the Navy list on Sept. 16, 1947; sold for scrapping on Oct. 30, 1947 to Lipsett of New York City and delivered on Dec. 5, 1947

Wyoming circa 1920s during normal fleet operations. NH 69504

Wyoming (AG-17) photographed circa 1935, after conversion to training ship. NH 90498

Arkansas, photo taken early in her career. NH 61691

1st Commanding Officer: Capt. R. C. Smith

Authorized: March 3, 1909

Keel Laid: Jan. 25, 1910

Launched: Jan. 14, 1911

Commissioned: Sept. 17, 1912

Sponsor: Miss Mary Louise Macon

Displacement Standard Tons: 26,000

Displacement Full Load Tons: 27,243

Design Crew Complement: 58 officers, 1005 enlisted, 1594 for war service, 1663 as Flagship

Main Guns: 12-12" 50 caliber (16,000-yard range with armor-piercing rounds)

Secondary Guns: 21-5" 51 caliber

Construction Costs: $6 million maximum plus armor and armament

Armor: Maximum thickness 12" at turret face plates

Length Overall: 554' waterline, 562' overall

Mean Draught: 28'6"

Extreme Beam: 93'3"

Torpedo Tubes: 2-21" submerged

Catapults: None

Builder: New York Shipbuilding Corporation, Camden, New Jersey

Original Engines Manufactured: New York Shipbuilding Parsons type; turbine

Original Boilers Manufactured: Babcock & Wilcox type; no. 12

Original Fuel: Coal, 2691 tons, and oil, 400 tons

Drive: Turbine drive, 4 screws

Sisters: *Wyoming* Class

Designed Speed: 21 knots

Designed Shaft Horsepower: 28,000

Design Comments: First-class Battleship, coal- and oil-fired boilers

History Highlights:

- 1912 with the Atlantic Fleet; Presidential naval review in the Hudson River on Oct. 14, 1912; transported President Taft to the Panama Canal Zone in December, 1912

- June 2, 1913 with the Atlantic Fleet; Mediterranean cruise October–December, 1913; April 24, 1914 occupation of Vera Cruz, Mexico

- WWI cruise, Atlantic coast; July 28, 1918 to 6th Battle Squadron of the British Grand Fleet; present at the surrender of the German High Seas Fleet on Nov. 20, 1918 at Scapa Flow

- 1919–1921 with the Pacific Fleet; 1921 Flagship Commander Battleship Force, Atlantic Fleet

- WWII Atlantic Fleet, escort and convoy duty, December, 1941 to April, 1944 (8 trips); June 6, 1944 D-Day support at Omaha Beach

- June 25, 1944 at Cherbourg, France; August 15, 1944 invasion of southern France; Nov. 8, 1944 to the Pacific Fleet

- Feb. 16–19, 1945 at Iwo Jima; March 25 to May 10, 1945 off Okinawa; Oct. 15, 1945 to Seattle, Washington

- October–December, 1945 troop transport duty with "Magic Carpet"

- During WWII *Arkansas* was the only battleship in the U.S. fleet with 12" guns—all others had 14" or 16" main battery armaments

Date Decommissioned: July 25, 1946 for use as a target ship of Operation Crossroads, Bikini Atoll tests (July 1 and 25, 1946)

Commendations: Four Battle Stars in WWII

Final Disposition: Used as Bikini Atoll atom bomb test and sunk July 25, 1946, near ground zero of "Baker test"

1st Commanding Officer: Capt. T. S. Rodgers

Authorized: June 24, 1910

Keel Laid: Sept. 11, 1911

Launched: Oct. 30, 1912

Commissioned: April 15, 1914

Sponsor: Miss Elsie Calder

Displacement Standard Tons: 27,000

Displacement Full Load Tons: 28,367

Design Crew Complement: 58 officers, 984 enlisted, 1612 for war service

Main Guns: 10-14" 45 caliber (18,000-yard range with armor-piercing rounds)

Secondary Guns: 21-5" 51 caliber

Construction Costs: $6 million maximum plus armor and armament

Armor: Maximum thickness 14" at turret face plates

Length Overall: 565' waterline, 573' overall

Mean Draught: 28'6"

Extreme Beam: 95'3"

Torpedo Tubes: 4-21" submerged

Catapults: None

Builder: New York Navy Yard, Brooklyn, New York

Original Engines Manufactured: New York Navy Yard type; vertical 4 cylinder triple expansion reciprocating

Original Boilers Manufactured: Babcock & Wilcox type; no. 14

Original Fuel: Coal, 2850 tons, and oil, 400 tons

Drive: Reciprocating, 2 screws

Sisters: *New York Class*

Designed Speed: 21 knots

Designed Shaft Horsepower: 28,100

Design Comments: First-class Battleship, coal- and oil-fired boilers

History Highlights:

- July, 1914 Vera Cruz, Mexico; December, 1917 to U.S. Battleship Division 9 with the 6th Battle Squadron of the British Grand Fleet in the North Sea
- Present at the surrender of German High Seas Fleet at Firth of Forth in Scapa Flow on Nov. 21, 1918
- 1919 to Pacific Fleet at San Diego; May 20, 1937 at the coronation of King George VI; 1935 to the Atlantic Fleet
- 1941 neutrality patrol; 1941 to WWII, convoy duty; Nov. 8, 1942 invasion of North Africa at Safi
- December, 1942 to June, 1944 convoy duty and gunnery training duty in Chesapeake Bay; June, 1944 training cruise
- Nov. 21, 1944 to the Pacific Fleet for gunnery training; January, 1945 at Pearl Harbor
- February, 1945 at Iwo Jima; March, 1945 at Okinawa; April 14, 1945 at Okinawa—damaged by kamikaze
- Transport duty to the West Coast; to New York from Pearl Harbor; arrived at New York on Oct. 19, 1945

Date Decommissioned: Operation Crossroads, Bikini atom bomb test #1; July 1, 1946, and test #2 on July 25, 1946; decommissioned at Kwajalein on August 29, 1946

Commendations: Three Battle Stars in WWII

Final Disposition: To Pearl Harbor in 1946 for a bomb test study from 1946 to 1948; towed 40 miles out to sea on July 8, 1948 and sunk after an eight-hour battle maneuver test

New York running trials, 1914 prior to her commissioning April 15, 1914. NH 45140

1st Commanding Officer: Capt. A. W. Grant

Authorized: June 24, 1910

Keel Laid: April 17, 1911

Launched: May 18, 1912

Commissioned: March 12, 1914

Sponsor: Miss Claudia Lyon

Displacement Standard Tons: 27,000 (modernized to 29,500)

Displacement Full Load Tons: 28,367 (modernized to 32,000)

Design Crew Complement: 58 officers, 994 enlisted, 1612 for war service

Main Guns: 10-14" 45 caliber (18,000- yard range with armor-piercing rounds)

Secondary Guns: 21-5" 51 caliber (modernized with 6-5"/ 51 caliber, 10-3" AA; 40-40 millimeter AA; 44-20 millimeter AA)

Construction Costs: $6 million maximum plus armor and armament

Armor: Maximum thickness 14" at turret face pates

Length Overall: 565 ' waterline, 573' overall

Mean Draught: 28'6"

Extreme Beam: 95'3"

Torpedo Tubes: 4-21" submerged

Catapults: None

Builder: Newport News Shipbuilding Co., Newport News, Virginia

Original Engines Manufactured: Newport News type; vertical 4 cylinder triple expansion reciprocating

Original Boilers Manufactured: Babcock & Wilcox type: WT; no. 14

Original Fuel: Coal, 2892 tons and oil, 400 tons

Drive: Reciprocating 2 screws (maximum propeller diameter 18'8")

Texas running standardization trials, Oct. 23, 1913, prior to her commissioning on March 12, 1914. NH 61713

Sisters: *New York* Class

Designed Speed: 21 knots

Designed Shaft Horsepower: 28,100

Design Comments: First-class Battleship; coal- and oil-fired boilers

History Highlights:
- Atlantic Fleet on March 24, 1914; Tampico incident at Vera Cruz, Mexico from June 21–22, 1914
- August 27, 1917 ran around at Block Island, New York; Feb. 11, 1918 with Battle Division 9 to the 6th Battleship Squadron of the British Grand Fleet
- Nov. 11, 1918 with the Grand Fleet during the surrender of the German High Seas Fleet; July 17, 1920 classified as BB-35
- 1919–1941 Atlantic and Pacific Fleets; Dec. 7, 1941 at Casco Bay, Maine; November, 1942 with the invasion of North Africa
- 1943 convoy duty with the Atlantic Fleet; June 6, 1944 off Point du Hoc, Normandy; June 25, 1944 damaged off Cherbourg, France
- November, 1944 to the Pacific Fleet; February, 1945 at Iwo Jima; March, 1945 at Okinawa
- May, 1945 to August 15, 1945 in the Philippines; September, 1945 to December, 1945 troop transport duty with Operation "Magic Carpet"
- Jan. 21, 1946 to the Norfolk Navy Yard; June, 1946 to Baltimore, Maryland; January, 1948 towed to San Jacinto State Park in Texas

Date Decommissioned: April 21, 1948 in San Jacinto Park; turned over to the State of Texas

Commendations: Five Battle Stars in World War II; Navy Occupation Service Medal Pacific

Final Disposition: Struck from the List on April 30, 1948; now serving as a Texas State memorial

Texas Memorial, a memorial since April 21, 1948 and shown in her new sliding collar anchorage in San Jacinto State Park, Laporte, Texas. Photo taken 1991. © COURTESY HUGH I. POWER, JR. REGISTRATION #VAU 155-735

USS Nevada
BB-36

1st Commanding Officer: Capt. W. S. Sims
Authorized: March 4, 1911
Keel Laid: Nov. 4, 1912
Launched: July 11, 1914
Commissioned: March 11, 1916
Sponsor: Miss Eleanor Anne Seibert
Displacement Standard Tons: 27,500
Displacement Full Load Tons: 28,400
Design Crew Complement: 55 officers, 809 enlisted, 1598 for war service
Main Guns: 10-14" 50 caliber (20,000- yard range with armor-piercing rounds)
Secondary Guns: 21-5" 51 caliber
Construction Costs: $6 million max + armor and armament
Armor: Maximum thickness 18" at turret face plates
Length Overall: 575 ' waterline, 583' overall
Mean Draught: 28'6"
Extreme Beam: 95'3"
Torpedo Tubes: 4-21" submerged
Catapults: None (added during later modifications)
Builder: Fore River Company, Quincy, Massachusetts
Original Engines Manufactured: Curtis (Fore River) type cruising turbine
Original Boilers Manufactured: Yarrow (Fore River) type WT; no. 12
Original Fuel: Oil, 2037 tons (611,100 gallons)

Nevada running trials, circa early 1916, prior to her commissioning on March 11, 1916. NH 45796

Nevada is sunk as a target off Hawaii on July 31, 1948 by naval gunfire and aerial torpedoes following the conclusion of tests conducted during her use in the Bikini atom bomb tests on July 1 and 25, 1946.

NATIONAL ARCHIVES PHOTOGRAPH 80-G-498282

Drive: Turbine drive, 4 screws
Sisters: *Nevada* Class
Designed Speed: 21 knots
Designed Shaft Horsepower: 26,500
Design Comments: First-class Battleship, oil-fired boilers
History Highlights:
- Atlantic Fleet May 26, 1916; August 23, 1918 to Bantry Bay, Ireland, to serve with the British Grand Fleet
- 1920–1940 Atlantic and Pacific Fleets; July to September, 1925 goodwill cruise to New Zealand and Australia
- Dec. 7, 1941 at Pearl Harbor, got under way but beached at Hospital Point, with 50 killed and 109 wounded during the attack
- Refloated on Feb. 12, 1942; fire support for the capture of the Attu in Alaska on May 11–18, 1942
- June, 1942–March, 1944 modernized at Norfolk; June 6–17 and June 25, 1944 at Normandy and Cherbourg; August 15 to Sept. 25, 1944 at the Invasion of southern France
- March 27, 1945 off Okinawa, hit by a kamikaze, killing 11; 2 were killed by shore battery on April 5, 1945
- At Okinawa from April to August, 1945; then to Japan and Occupation duty in Tokyo Bay
- Used in Operation Crossroads Bikini atoll atom bomb tests July 1 and July 25, 1946—survived these tests

Date Decommissioned: At Pearl Harbor on August 29, 1946
Commendations: Seven World War II Battle Stars
Final Disposition: Sunk by naval gunfire and aerial torpedoes off Hawaii on July 31, 1948

· ·

Oklahoma off Brest, France, Dec. 13, 1918, while escorting President Wilson's transport, *George Washington.* Note the Brest pilot boat. NH 57233

1st Commanding Officer: Capt. R. Welles

Authorized: March 4, 1911

Keel Laid: Oct. 26, 1912

Launched: March 23, 1914

Commissioned: May 2, 1916 at Philadelphia

Sponsor: Miss Lorena J. Cruce

Displacement Standard Tons: 27,500

Displacement Full Load Tons: 28,400

Design Crew Complement: 55 officers, 809 enlisted, 1598 for war service

Main Guns: 10-14" 50 caliber (20,000 yard-range with armor-piercing rounds)

Secondary Guns: 21-5" 51 caliber

Construction Costs: $6 million maximum plus armor and armament

Armor: Maximum thickness 18" at turret face plates

Length Overall: 575' 583' overall

Mean Draught: 28'6"

Extreme Beam: 95'3"

Torpedo Tubes: 4-21" submerged

Catapults: None (added during later modifications)

Builder: New York Shipbuilding Corporation, Camden, New Jersey

Original Engines Manufactured: New York Shipbuilding type; vertical 4 cylinder triple expansion reciprocating

Original Boilers Manufactured: Babcock & Wilcox type: WT; no. 12

Original Fuel: Oil, 2037 tons (611,100 gallons)

Drive: Reciprocating, 2 screws

Sisters: *Nevada* Class

Designed Speed: 21 knots

Designed Shaft Horsepower: 24,800

Design Comments: First-class Battleship; oil-fired boilers

History Highlights:

· To the Atlantic Fleet, 1916; August 13, 1918 convoy duty of Allied convoys in European waters

· June 15, 1919 part of the escort group for President Wilson on the liner *George Washington*

· 1919 with Atlantic Fleet; twice to South American waters in the Pacific

· Early in 1921, combined fleet exercise with the Pacific Fleet

· 1921 to the Pacific Fleet; 1925 Pacific Fleet; Battle fleet cruise to Australia and New Zealand

· To Spain during the outbreak of Civil War on July 24, 1936; to Pearl Harbor on Dec. 6, 1940

· December 7, 1941 at Pearl Harbor; capsized with 415 killed; with Julio Castro and others 32 were saved through bottom of ship

· Salvage began in March of 1943 and the *Oklahoma* entered drydock on Dec. 28, 1943

Date Decommissioned: At Pearl Harbor on Sept. 1, 1944; stripped of guns and superstructure; sold to Moore Drydock of Oakland, California

Commendations: One WWII Battle Star

Final Disposition: En route to Oakland on May 17, 1947, 540 miles outbound from Pearl Harbor, the towline parted and the *Oklahoma* sank

1st Commanding Officer: Capt. H. B. Wilson

Authorized: August 22, 1912

Keel Laid: Oct. 27, 1913

Launched: March 16, 1915

Commissioned: June 12, 1916

Sponsor: Miss Elizabeth Kolb

Displacement Standard Tons: 31,400 (modernized to 33,100)

Displacement Full Load Tons: 32,657 (modernized to 40,300)

Design Crew Complement: 55 officers, 860 enlisted, 1574 for war service

Main Guns: 12-14" 45 caliber MK3 (18,000 yard-range with armor-piercing rounds)

Secondary Guns: 22-5" 51 caliber MK15 (modernized with 16-5"/38 caliber; 10-40 millimeter AA; 51-20 millimeter AA)

Construction Costs: $7.4 million maximum plus armor and armament

Armor: Maximum thickness 18" at turret face plates

Length Overall: 600 ' waterline, 608' overall

Mean Draught: 28'10"

Extreme Beam: 97'1" (modernized to 100')

Torpedo Tubes: 4-21" submerged

Catapults: None (added during later modifications)

Builder: Newport News Shipbuilding Co., Newport News, Virginia

Original Engines Manufactured: Curtis (Newport News) type; turbine

Original Boilers Manufactured: Babcock & Wilcox type: WT; no. 12

Original Fuel: Oil, 2322 tons (694,830 gallons); modernized to 5870 tons (1,761,000 gallons)

Drive: Turbine drive, 4 screws (maximum propeller diameter 12'7")

Pennsylvania at Hampton Roads, Virginia on Dec. 10, 1916 six months after commissioning. NH 63562

Pennsylvania is scuttled off Kwajalein on Feb. 10, 1948 following the conclusion of tests conducted during her use in the Bikini atom bomb tests on July 1 and 25, 1946.

Sisters: *Pennsylvania* Class

Designed Speed: 21 knots

Designed Shaft Horsepower: 31,500 (modernized to 35,000)

Design Comments: First-class Battleship; oil-fired boilers

History Highlights:

- Oct. 12, 1916 Flagship Commander-in-Chief Atlantic Fleet; WWI fleet maneuvers with the Atlantic Fleet; Dec. 4, 1918 to Brest, France, with President Wilson
- 1919–1922 Atlantic and Pacific Fleet maneuvers; August 22, 1922 to the Pacific Fleet till 1929 for overhaul and modernization
- August 31 to December, 1941 with the Pacific Fleet; Dec. 7, 1941 in drydock at Pearl Harbor; 15 killed, 14 missing and 38 wounded
- April, 1943, Aleutian campaign; November, 1943 Gilbert Islands; January, 1944, Kwajalein Islands
- June, 1944 Marianas Islands; July, 1944, Guam
- Oct. 24–25, 1944 Battle of Surigao Strait, Japanese Battleships *Fuso* and *Yamashiro* sunk
- January, 1945 in the South China Sea
- August 12, 1945 Buckner Bay, Okinawa, 20 killed and 10 wounded; 3 of 4 propeller shafts were severely damaged from a torpedo hit to the starboard side near the stern; out of service balance of WWII

Date Decommissioned: Bikini bomb tests on July 1 and 25, 1946; decommissioned on August 29, 1946 at Kwajalein Lagoon

Commendations: Eight WWII Battle Stars; WWII Navy Unit commendation

Final Disposition: Scuttled off Kwajalein Island on Feb. 10, 1948; struck from the Navy list on Feb. 19, 1948

1st Commanding Officer: Capt. J. D. McDonald

Authorized: March 4, 1913

Keel Laid: March 16, 1914

Launched: June 19, 1915

Commissioned: Oct. 17, 1916

Sponsor: Miss Esther Ross

Displacement Standard Tons: 31,400 (modernized to 32,600)

Displacement Full Load Tons: 32,567 (modernized to 37,654)

Design Crew Complement: 55 officers, 860 enlisted, 1620 for war service

Main Guns: 12-14" 45 caliber MK3 (18,000-yard range with armor-piercing rounds)

Secondary Guns: 22-5" 51 caliber; 4-3" 50 caliber (modernized with 10-5"/51 MK 15; 8-5" 25 MK11; 80-50 caliber/63.8

Construction Costs: $7.425 million plus armor and armament

Armor: Maximum thickness 18" at turret face plates

Length Overall: 600 ' waterline, 608' overall

Mean Draught: 28'10"

Extreme Beam: 97'1" (modernized to 106' 2 /34")

Torpedo Tubes: 2-21" submerged

Catapults: None (added at later modifications)

Builder: New York Navy Yard, Brooklyn, New York

Original Engines Manufactured: Parsons (New York Navy Yard) type; turbine

Original Boilers Manufactured: Babcock & Wilcox type: WT; no. 12

Original Fuel: Oil, 2322 tons (694,830 gallons), modernized to 4630 tons (1,389,000 gallons)

Drive: Turbine drive, 4 screws (maximum propeller diameter 12'7")

Sisters: *Pennsylvania* Class

Arizona Memorial at Pearl Harbor in Honolulu, Hawaii.   COURTESY OF USS *ARIZONA* MEMORIAL COLLECTION, NATIONAL PARK SERVICE

Arizona circa 1917, within a short time after her Oct. 17, 1916 commissioning. NH 67586

Designed Speed: 21 knots

Designed Shaft Horsepower: 34,000, modernized to 35,081)

Design Comments: First-class Battleship, oil-fired boilers

History Highlights:

- October, 1916 with the Atlantic Fleet; WWI training in Chesapeake Bay
- Nov. 18, 1918 with naval force in British waters; April–July, 1919 Mediterranean cruise
- 1918–1921 with the Atlantic Fleet; 1921–1929 with the Pacific Fleet
- 1931 carried Herbert Hoover on a cruise to the West Indies
- 1931–1941 with the Pacific Fleet for normal Fleet maneuvers and Fleet problems
- Dec. 7, 1941 at Pearl Harbor; she took eight bomb hits; one bomb hit near the forward magazine

- Bomb hit near the forward magazine caused a fire which caused black powder to ignite; smokeless powder magazine explosion
- Powder magazine explosion completely wrecked the forward section of the ship, killing Capt. Franklin van Valkenburg, Rear Admiral Isaac Kidd and 1104 of the Arizona's crew

Date Decommissioned: Sunk Dec. 7, 1941, not raised; on Dec. 1, 1942 stricken from the Navy list

Commendations: One WWII Battle Star

Final Disposition: Unofficial Memorial on March 7, 1950; U.S. Congress approved Memorial on March 15, 1958; Memorial completed on May 30, 1962 for all military personnel killed in the Pearl Harbor attack

Arizona as she rested on the bottom in Pearl Harbor, Dec. 10, 1941. NH 63918

1st Commanding Officer: Capt. A. H. Robertson

Authorized: June 30, 1914

Keel Laid: Oct. 14, 1915

Launched: April 13, 1917

Commissioned: May 20, 1918

Sponsor: Miss Margaret C. De Baca

Displacement Standard Tons: 32,000

Displacement Full Load Tons: 33,000

Design Crew Complement: 58 officers, 1026 enlisted, 1560 for war service

Main Guns: 12-14" 50 caliber MK IV (34,000-yard range with armor-piercing rounds)

Secondary Guns: 14-5" 51 caliber; 4-3" 50 caliber (modernized during WWII with increased AA fire support)

Construction Costs: $7.8 million maximum plus armor and armament

Armor: Maximum thickness 18" at turret face plates

Length Overall: 600' waterline, 624' overall

Mean Draught: 30'

Extreme Beam: 97'5"

Torpedo Tubes: 2-21" submerged

Catapults: None (added at later modifications)

Builder: New York Navy Yard, Brooklyn, New York

Original Engines Manufactured: Curtiss Turbine General Electric Drive

Original Boilers Manufactured: Babcock & Wilcox type: WT; no. 9

Original Fuel: Oil, 3277 tons (983,100 gallons)

Drive: Turbo-electric, 4 screws

Sisters: *New Mexico* Class

Designed Speed: 21 knots

Designed Shaft Horsepower: 27,500

Design Comments: First-class Battleship, oil-fired boilers

History Highlights:

- Jan. 15, 1919 to Brest, France, to escort President Wilson's return from the Versailles Peace Conference
- July 16, 1919 Flagship, Pacific Fleet; 1919–1931 Fleet maneuvers with Atlantic and Pacific Fleets
- January, 1933 to October, 1934 Atlantic Fleet; October, 1934 to December, 1940 Pacific Fleet; May, 1941 Pacific Fleet at Pearl Harbor; May, 1941 to the Atlantic Fleet
- January, 1942 to the Pacific Fleet; May, 1943 to Adak, Alaska to expel the Japanese; November, 1943 invasion of the Gilberts
- January, 1944 invasion of the Marshall Islands; June, 1944 bombarded Tinian, Saipan and Guam
- Jan 2–6, 1945 damaged during the invasion of Luzon during fire support
- May 12, 1945 damaged by kamikaze with 54 killed and 199 wounded
- At Tokyo Bay on Sept. 2, 1945 during Japanese surrender ceremonies

Date Decommissioned: To Boston on Oct. 17, 1945; decommissioned on July 7, 1946

Commendations: Six WWII Battle Stars

Final Disposition: Stricken from the Navy list on Oct. 13, 1947; sold for scrapping to Lipsett, Inc., New York City

Below: Battleships at Pearl Harbor on Dec. 17, 1943. (l-r): *Idaho* (BB-42), *New Mexico* (BB-40), *Mississippi* (BB-41). Photographed from *Natoma Bay* (CVE-62). A rare picture of the three ships of the *New Mexico* class at one anchorage.
NATIONAL ARCHIVES PHOTOGRAPH 80-G-275940

Above: *New Mexico* off New York City during the fleet review on Dec. 27, 1918, seven months after commissioning. NH 45491

Mississippi (EAG-128, ex-BB-41) fires a "terrier" surface-to-air missile during at-sea tests, circa 1953–55.
NATIONAL ARCHIVES PHOTOGRAPH 80-G-K-17878

Mississippi anchored off New York city for the World War I "Victory Fleet Review" on Dec. 25, 1917, seven days after commissioning.
NH 46047

1st Commanding Officer: Capt. J. L. Lane

Authorized: June 30, 1914

Keel Laid: April 5, 1915

Launched: Jan. 25, 1917

Commissioned: Dec. 18, 1917

Sponsor: Miss Camelle McBeath

Displacement Standard Tons: 32,000

Displacement Full Load Tons: 33,000

Design Crew Complement: 55 officers, 1026 enlisted, 1600 for war service

Main Guns: 12-14" 50 caliber, MK IV (34,000-yard range with armor-piercing rounds)

Secondary Guns: 14-5" 51 caliber; 4-3" 50 caliber (modified during WWII with increased AA fire support)

Construction Costs: $7.8 million maximum plus armor and armament

Armor: Maximum thickness 18" at turret face plates

Length Overall: 600 ' waterline, 624' overall

Mean Draught: 30'

Extreme Beam: 97'5"

Torpedo Tubes: 2-21" submerged

Catapults: none (added at later modifications)

Builder: Newport News Shipbuilding Co., Newport News, Virginia

Original Engines Manufactured: Curtis (Newport News) cruising turbines

Original Boilers Manufactured: Babcock & Wilcox type: WT; no. 9

Original Fuel: Oil, 3277 tons (983,100 gallons)

Drive: Turbine drive, 4 screws

Sisters: *New Mexico* Class

Designed Speed: 21 knots

Designed Shaft Horsepower: 32,000

Design Comments: First-class Battleship; oil-fired boilers; modernized from March 30, 1931 to Sept. 1, 1933

History Highlights:

- January, 1918 to July, 1919 Atlantic Fleet; July, 1919 to Pacific Fleet at San Pedro, California
- June 12, 1924 off San Pedro; main #2 turret explosion killed 48 men
- March 30, 1931 to Sept. 1, 1933 at Norfolk Navy Yard for modernization overhaul; 1934–1941 Pacific Fleet
- June 15, 1941 to Dec. 9, 1941 Atlantic Fleet convoys; Dec. 9, 1941 to Sept. 6, 1945 Pacific Fleet; May 10, 1943 Aleutian Islands
- Nov. 20, 1943 a turret explosion killed 43 men during the bombardment of Makin Island
- Jan. 31, 1944 Marshall Islands; Sept. 12, 1944 Palau Islands; October, 1944 Battle of Suriago Strait
- June 5, 1945 kamikaze hits starboard side; Sept. 2, 1945 in Tokyo Bay to witness the signing of the surrender document
- Converted to AG-128 on Feb 15, 1946, later to EAG-128; Prototype for later conversions to *Iowa* Class

Date Decommissioned: Decommissioned as BB-41 on Feb 2, 1946; decommissioned as EAG-128 on Sept. 17, 1956

Commendations: Eight WWII Battle Stars; WWII Navy Unit Commendation

Final Disposition: Sold for scrap to Bethlehem Steel on Nov. 28, 1956

1st Commanding Officer: Capt. C. T. Vogelgesang

Authorized: June 30, 1914

Keel Laid: Jan. 20, 1915

Launched: June 30, 1917

Commissioned: March 24, 1919

Sponsor: Miss H. A. Limons

Displacement Standard Tons: 32,000

Displacement Full Load Tons: 33,000

Design Crew Complement: 55 officers, 1026 enlisted, 1600 for war service

Main Guns: 12-14" 50 caliber MK IV (34,000-yard range with armor-piercing rounds)

Secondary Guns: 14-5" 51 caliber; 4-3" 50 caliber (modified during WWII with increased AA fire support)

Construction Costs: $7.8 million maximum plus armor and armament

Armor: Maximum thickness 18" at turret face plates

Length Overall: 600 ' waterline, 624' overall

Mean Draught: 30'

Extreme Beam: 97'50"

Torpedo Tubes: 2-21" submerged

Catapults: None (added during later modifications)

Builder: New York Shipbuilding Co., Camden, New Jersey

Original Engines Manufactured: Parsons (New York Shipbuilding) cruising turbines

Original Boilers Manufactured: Babcock & Wilcox type:WT; no. 9

Original Fuel: oil, 3277 tons (983,100 gallons)

Drive: 21 knots

Sisters: *New Mexico* Class

Designed Speed: 21 knots

Designed Shaft Horsepower: 32,000

Design Comments: First-class Battleship,; oil-fired boilers

History Highlights:

- September, 1919 Pacific Fleet; Sept. 13, 1919 Fleet review by President Wilson
- 1919–1931 Pacific Fleet; 1931–1934 modernization; 1934 to June 6, 1941 with Pacific Fleet
- June, 1941 to Dec. 9, 1941 Atlantic Fleet; January, 1942–1945 Pacific Fleet; April 7, 1943 Aleutian Islands
- November, 1943 Gilbert Islands; January, 1944 Kwajalein; June, 1944 Saipan
- June, 1944, Guam; September, 1944 Peleiu (Philippines); Oct. 22, 1944 at Bremerton for repairs
- Feb. 14–March 7, 1945 Iwo Jima; March, 1945–April, 1945 Okinawa
- August 27, 1945 in Tokyo Bay; witnessed the signing on the *Missouri* of the Japanese Surrender, Sept. 2, 1945; departing Sept. 6, 1945
- Nov. 16, 1945 to the Norfolk Navy Yard

Date Decommissioned: Decommissioned July 3, 1946; in reserve until Nov. 24, 1947

Commendations: Seven WWII Battle Stars

Final Disposition: Stricken and sold for scrap on Nov. 24, 1947 to Lipsett Inc. of New York City

Idaho, photographed on June 23, 1919 three months after commissioning. NH 59955

Tennessee, photographed Feb. 26, 1921, eight months after commissioning.
NH 63416

1st Commanding Officer: Capt. R. H. Leigh

Authorized: March 3, 1915

Keel Laid: May 14, 1917

Launched: April 30, 1919

Commissioned: June 3, 1920

Sponsor: Miss Helen Lenore Roberts

Displacement Standard Tons: 32,300

Displacement Full Load Tons: 33,190 (modernized to 40,400)

Design Crew Complement: 57 officers, 1026 enlisted, 1407 for war service

Main Guns: 12-14" 50 caliber MK IV (34,000-yard range with armor-piercing rounds)

Secondary Guns: 14-5" 51 caliber; 4-3" 50 caliber (modernization with 15-5"/38 caliber dual purpose; 10-4 millimeter QUAD AA; 43-60 20 millimeter AA)

Construction Costs: $7.8 million maximum plus armor and armament

Armor: Maximum thickness 18" at turret face plates

Length Overall: 600 ' waterline, 624'6" overall

Mean Draught: 30'3"

Extreme Beam: 97'4", modernized to 114'

Torpedo Tubes: 2-21" submerged

Catapults: None (added at later modifications)

Builder: New York Navy Yard, Brooklyn, New York

Original Engines Manufactured: Westinghouse geared turbines

Original Boilers Manufactured: Babcock & Wilcox type: WT; no. 8

Original Fuel: Oil, 4893 tons (1,467,900 gallons)

Drive: Turbo-electric, 4 screws

Sisters: *Tennessee* Class

Designed Speed: 21 knots

Designed Shaft Horsepower: 26,800 (modernized to 29,000)

Design Comments: First-class Battleship; oil-fired boilers; guns elevation to 30 degrees; *Tennessee* BB-43 and up with "post Jutland hull design" also main battery and secondary with fire control

History Highlights:

- 1920 Atlantic Fleet shakedown and fit; June 17, 1921 to Pacific Fleet at San Pedro, California
- 1921–1941 Pacific Fleet training and Fleet exercises; Dec. 7, 1941 at Pearl Harbor
- August 27, 1942 to May 7, 1943 modernization at Puget Sound; August 1, 1943 in the Aleutians—bombarded Kiska; November, 1943 Betio Island campaign
- January, 1944 at Kwajalein Island; Feb. 17, 1944 at Enewetok Island; March 20, 1944 at Kavieng Island
- June, 1944 off Saipan; June 14, 1944 at Tinian, hit in the side and aft by shore battery of 4.7" guns
- September, 1944 off the Philippines; Oct. 21, 1944 stern damaged by transport *Warhawk* (AP-168)
- Oct. 24–25, 1944 Battle of Surigao Strait; Japanese Battleships *Fuso* and *Yamashiro* sunk; February, 1945 off Iwo Jima; March, 1945 off Okinawa
- April 12, 1945 hit off Okinawa by "Val" near bridge with 22 killed and 107 injured

Date Decommissioned: Dec. 7, 1945 mothballed at Philadelphia; decommissioned on Feb 14, 1947

Commendations: Ten WWII Battle Stars; WWII Unit Commendation

Final Disposition: March 1, 1959 stricken from the Navy List; July 10, 1959 sold to Bethlehem Steel for scrapping.

California leaving Mare Island Navy Yard, California, upon completion in August, 1921.
NH 70815

1st Commanding Officer: Capt. H. J. Ziegemeier

Authorized: March 3, 1915

Keel Laid: Oct. 25, 1916

Launched: Nov. 20, 1919

Commissioned: August 10, 1921

Sponsor: Mrs. R. T. Zane

Displacement Standard Tons: 32,600

Displacement Full Load Tons: 33,190 (modernized to 40,400)

Design Crew Complement: 57 officers, 1026 enlisted, 1407 for war service

Main Guns: 12-14" 50 caliber MK IV (34,000-yard range with armor-piercing rounds)

Secondary Guns: 14-5" 51 caliber 4-3" 50 caliber (modernized with 16-5"/38 caliber dual purpose 10-40 millimeter quad AA 43-60 20 millimeter AA)

Construction Costs: $7.8 million maximum plus armor and armament

Armor: Maximum thickness 18" at turret face plates

Length Overall: 600' waterline, 624'6" overall

Mean Draught: 31 maximum

Extreme Beam: 97'4", modernized to 114'

Torpedo Tubes: 2-21" submerged

Catapults: None (added at later modifications)

Builder: Mare Island Navy Yard, Vallejo, California

Original Engines Manufactured: General Electric geared turbines

Original Boilers Manufactured: Bureau Express no. 8

Original Fuel: Oil 4656 tons (1,396,800 gallons; modernized to 4893 tons, 1,467,900 gallons)

Drive: Turbo-electric 4-screws

Sisters: *Tennessee* Class

Designed Speed: 21 knots

Designed Shaft Horsepower: 28,500

Design Comments: First-class Battleship; oil-fired boilers

History Highlights:

· September, 1921 to Pacific Fleet as Flagship; 1921–1941 Flagship of Pacific Fleet and Flagship of Battle Fleet Battleship Force, U.S. Fleet

· 1940 with Fleet to Pearl Harbor; Dec. 7, 1941 at Pearl Harbor; 94 killed, 51 wounded in the battle

· Dec. 7, 1941 sunk to superstructure; March 25, 1942 refloated with repair at Pearl Harbor and Bremerton, Washington until Jan. 31, 1944

· June, 1944 at Saipan; shell hit, killed 1 and wounded 9; August, 1944 collision with the *Tennessee* (BB-43)

· Oct. 24 to 25, 1944 Battle of Surigao Strait; Japanese Battleships *Fuso* and *Yamashiro* were sunk

· January, 1945 at Luzon in the Philippines; Jan. 6, 1945 hit by kamikaze—44 killed, 155 wounded; June 15, 1945 at Okinawa

· July, 1945 in the East Chine Sea on mine-sweeping duty; September and October, 1945 with the 6th Army occupation landing Honshu

· Returned to Philadelphia on Dec. 7, 1945

Date Decommissioned: In commission in reserve August 7, 1946; out of commission in reserve on Feb. 14, 1947

Commendations: Seven WWII Battle Stars

Final Disposition: Stricken from the Navy List on Feb. 24, 1959; sold for scrapping on July 10, 1959

USS Colorado
BB-45

1st Commanding Officer: Capt. R. R. Belknap

Authorized: August 29, 1916

Keel Laid: May 29, 1919

Launched: March 22, 1921

Commissioned: August 30, 1923

Sponsor: Mrs. M. Melville

Displacement Standard Tons: 32,600

Displacement Full Load Tons: 33,590 (modernized to 39,400)

Design Crew Complement: 58 officers, 1022 enlisted

Main Guns: 8-16" 45 caliber MK I (34,500-yard range with armor-piercing rounds)AP)

Secondary Guns: 12-5" 51 caliber; 8-3" 50 caliber (modernized with 8-5"/51 caliber; 8-5"/25 dual purpose; 8-40 millimeter; QUAD AA 2-40 millimeter TWIN 44-46 20 millimeter AA)

Construction Costs: $11,500,000 maximum plus armor and armament

Armor: Maximum thickness 18" at turret face plates

Length Overall: 600' waterline, 624'6" overall

Mean Draught: 30'6"

Extreme Beam: 97'6" (modernized to 108')

Torpedo Tubes: 2-21" submerged

Catapults: None; 2 after commissioning

Builder: New York Shipbuilding Corporation, Camden, New Jersey

Original Engines Manufactured: Westinghouse geared turbines

Original Boilers Manufactured: Babcock & Wilcox type: WT; no. 8

Original Fuel: Oil, 4570 tons (1,371,000 gallons); modernized to 5392 tons (1,617,600 gallons)

Colorado off Camden, New Jersey on Oct. 10, 1923, two months after commissioning. NH 55277

Drive: Turbo-electric, 4 screws

Sisters: *Colorado* Class

Designed Speed: 21 knots

Designed Shaft Horsepower: 28,900 (modernized to 31,400)

Design Comments: First-Class Battleship; oil-fired boilers

History Highlights:

- Dec. 29, 1923; maiden voyage shakedown cruise to England and France; to the Pacific Fleet on Sept. 15, 1924
- 1924–1941 with the Pacific Battle Fleet; earthquake relief at Long Beach, California March 10 and 11, 1933
- June 11 to July 22, 1937 helped search for Amelia Earhart; to Pearl Harbor on Jan. 27, 1941
- July, 1941 to March 31, 1942 at Puget Sound for overhaul; was here during attack on Pearl Harbor
- Nov. 8, 1942 to Sept. 17, 1943 near Fiji Islands and New Hebrides Islands; October, 1943 at Tarawa; January, 1944 at Marshall Islands
- May, 1944 Saipan, Guam, Tinian; July 24, 1944 hit 22 times from shore; Nov. 27, 1944 two kamikaze hits killed 19 and injured 72
- Jan. 9, 1945 accidental (friendly) gunfire killed 18 and wounded 51; March, 1945 invasion of Okinawa
- August, 1945 supported the occupation landing at Atsugi Airfield, Tokyo, Japan; Oct. 15, 1945 to San Francisco and to Seattle on Oct. 27, 1945; November, 1945 assigned to "Magic Carpet" duty

Date Decommissioned: To Bremerton for in activation; out of commission in reserve on Jan. 7, 1947

Commendations: Seven WWII Battle Stars

Final Disposition: Stricken from the Navy List on March 1, 1959; sold for scrapping on July 23, 1959

Pacific fleet firing. The big five at battle practice: *Colorado* (BB-45), *Maryland* (BB-46), *West Virginia* (BB-48), *Tennessee* (BB-43), and *California* (BB-44), circa 1930s. NH 63634

Maryland ready for launching, at Newport News, Virginia, on March 20, 1920, a typical stage of completion for a battleship to be launched. Two tankers and another large ship are also under construction on nearby slips. NH 93536

1st Commanding Officer: Capt. C. F. Preston

Authorized: August 29, 1916

Keel Laid: April 24, 1917

Launched: March 20, 1920

Commissioned: July 21, 1921

Sponsor: Mrs. E. Brooke Lee

Displacement Standard Tons: 32,600

Displacement Full Load Tons: 33,590 (moderized to 39,400)

Design Crew Complement: 62 officers, 1022 enlisted

Main Guns: 8-16" 45 caliber MK I (34,500-yard range with armor-piercing rounds)

Secondary Guns: 12-5" 51 caliber; 8-3" 50 caliber (modernized with 8-5"/51; 8-5"/25 caliber dual purpose; 8-40 millimeter QUAD AA; 2-40 millimeter Twin AA; 44-46 20 millimeter AA)

Construction Costs: $11,500 maximum plus armor and armament

Armor: Maximum thickness 18"at turret face plates

Length Overall: 600' waterline, 624' overall

Mean Draught: 30'6"

Extreme Beam: 97'6" (modernized to 108')

Torpedo Tubes: 2-21" submerged

Catapults: None; 2 after commissioning

Builder: Newport News Shipbuilding Co., Newport News, Virginia

Original Engines Manufactured: General Electric Drive Curtis turbines

Original Boilers Manufactured: Babcock & Wilcox type: WT; no. 8

Original Fuel: Oil, 4570 tons (1,371,000 gallons); modernized to 5392 tons (1,617,600 gallons)

Drive: Turbo-electric, 4 screws

Sisters: *Colorado* Class

Designed Speed: 21 knots

Designed Shaft Horsepower: 28,900 (modernized to 31,400)

Design Comments: First-class Battleship; oil-fired boilers; first U.S Battleship with 16" guns and new type sea-plane catapult

Maryland, photo taken around 1959 while awaiting scrapping, at Alameda, California 38 years after launching. NH 50170

History Highlights:
- At the 1922 Naval Academy graduation; 1925 at Brazil's centennial; September, 1925 voyage to Australia and New Zealand
- 1930s training with the Pacific Fleet; to Pearl Harbor in June 41; at Pearl Harbor on Dec. 7, 1941
- Repaired at Puget Sound until February, 1942; in Hawaiian waters as a backup during the Battle of Midway
- WWII amphibious force fire support ship; June 22, 1944 off Saipan; torpedo hit the bow on the port side
- Oct. 24 and 25, 1944 Battle of Surigao Strait; Japanese Battleships *Fuso* and *Yamashiro* were sunk

- On Nov. 29, 1944 31 were killed when a kamikaze attack damaged the area between turrets 1 and 2
- April 7, 1945 battle damage to #3 turret; May 7, 1945 to Bremerton for overhaul
- August 45 "Magic Carpet" duty

Date Decommissioned: April 15, 1946 Puget Sound in commission in reserve; April 3, 1947 at Bremerton in the Pacific Reserve Fleet

Commendations: Seven WWII Battle Stars

Final Disposition: Stricken from the Navy list of Feb. 24, 1959; sold for scrapping on July 8, 1959 to Learner Co. of Oakland, California

Maryland, probably running trials, in 1921, prior to her July 21, 1921 commissioning.
NH 46416

Artist's conception by F. Miller, drawn about 1916 before the design was finally decided for the four-ship *Colorado* class. *Washington* (BB-47) would have looked like her sister ships and the artist's conception had she been completed. *Colorado* (BB-45), *Maryland* (BB-46), *Washington* (BB-47), *West Virginia* (BB-48). NH 55271

1st Commanding Officer:
Authorized: August 29, 1916
Keel Laid: June 30, 1919
Launched: Sept. 1, 1921
Commissioned: Cancelled Feb. 8, 1922
Sponsor: Miss Jean Summers
Displacement Standard Tons: 32,600
Displacement Full Load Tons: 33,590
Design Crew Complement: 62 officers, 1022 enlisted
Main Guns: Assigned 8-16" 45 MK I
Secondary Guns: Assigned 20-5"; 8-3"
Construction Costs: $11.5 million maximum plus armor and armament
Armor: Maximum thickness 18" at turret face plates
Length Overall: 624'
Mean Draught: 30'6"
Extreme Beam: 97'6"
Torpedo Tubes: 2-21" submerged
Catapults: None
Builder: New York Shipbuilding Corporation, Camden, New Jersey
Original Engines Manufactured: Westinghouse geared turbines
Original Boilers Manufactured: Babcock & Wilcox type: WT; no. 8
Original Fuel: Oil, 4570 tons (1,371,000 gallons)
Drive: Turbo-electric, 4 screws
Sisters: *Colorado* Class
Designed Speed: 21 knots
Designed Shaft Horsepower: 28,000

Design Comments:
History Highlights:
· Cancelled by Washington Naval Treaty of Feb 8, 1922 when 75.9 percent complete
Date Decommissioned:
Commendations:
Final Disposition: Sunk on Nov. 25, 1924 as a gunnery target ship to test new torpedo blisters and other armor of new Battleships at the time

Washington under construction at the New York Shipbuilding Corporation in Camden, New Jersey on April 5, 1922. The ship was cancelled before completion. She was later used as a gunnery target ship and sunk on Nov. 25, 1924. NH 61244

West Virginia photographed on Dec. 18, 1923, 17 days after commissioning. (The last American dreadnought built.)
NH 43873

1st Commanding Officer: Capt. T. J. Senn

Authorized: August 29, 1916

Keel Laid: April 12, 1920

Launched: Nov. 17, 1921

Commissioned: Dec. 1, 1923

Sponsor: Miss Alice Wright Mann

Displacement Standard Tons: 32,600

Displacement Full Load Tons: 33,590 (modernized to 39,400)

Design Crew Complement: 62 officers, 1022 enlisted

Main Guns: 8-16" 45 caliber MK I (34,500 yards-range with armor-piercing shells)

Secondary Guns: 12-5" 51 caliber; 8-3" 50 caliber (modernized with 8-5"/38 caliber; 8-40 millimeter QUAD AA; 2-40 millimeter TWIN AA 44-46 millimeter AA)

Construction Costs: $11.5 million maximum plus armor and armament

Armor: Maximum thickness 18" at turret face plates

Length Overall: 624'

Mean Draught: 30'6"

Extreme Beam: 97'6" (modernized to 108')

Torpedo Tubes: 2-21" submerged

Catapults: None; 2 after commissioning

Builder: Newport News Shipbuilding Co., Newport News, Virginia

Original Engines Manufactured: General Electric Drive Curtis turbines

Original Boilers Manufactured: Babcock & Wilcox type: WT; no. 8

Original Fuel: Oil, 4570 tons (1,372,000 gallons); modernized to 5392 tons (1,617,600 gallons)

Drive: Turbo-electric, 4 screws

Sisters: *Colorado* Class

Designed Speed: 21 knots

Designed Shaft Horsepower: 28,900 (modernized to 31,400)

Design Comments: First-class Battleship; oil-fired boilers

History Highlights:

- 1923 to the Atlantic Fleet; June 16, 1924 grounded in Lynnhaven Channel due to defective rudder control
- Oct. 30, 1924 Flagship Battleship Division Battle Fleet; 1925 to Pacific and Atlantic/Pacific Fleet exercises
- 1939 to Pacific Fleet; 1940 to Pearl Harbor; on Dec. 7, 1941 takes seven torpedo hits and two bombs and sunk on an even keel
- Refloated on May 17, 1942 and repaired at Puget Sound; Oct. 5, 1944 Flagship Battleship Division 4; October, 1944 off Leyte in the Philippines
- Oct. 24 and 25 Battle of Surigao Straight; Japanese Battleships *Fuso* and *Yamashiro* are sunk
- December, 1944 off Palaus and Mindoro; January, 1944 at San Fernando Point; February, 1944 at Iwo Jima
- March, 1945 off Okinawa; April 1, 1945 hit by kamikaze at secondary battery #2—4 killed and 7 hurt
- Sept. 2, 1945 in Tokyo Bay to witness the Japanese surrender ceremonies; October–December, 1945 "Magic Carpet" duty

Date Decommissioned: Inactivated in February, 1946 at Seattle; decommissioned on Jan. 9, 1947

Commendations: Five WWII Battle Stars; ship's artifacts are at the University of West Virginia in Morgantown, also in Clarksburg and other sites throughout West Virginia

Final Disposition: Struck from the Navy list on March 1, 1959; sold for scrapping on August 24, 1959 to Union Mineral and Alloys Co. of New York City

Pearl Harbor attack, Dec. 7, 1941. View looking towards Battleship Row soon after the attack began (lower left to upper right): *Nevada* (BB-36), *Vestal* (AR-4) alongside *Arizona* (BB-39), *West Virginia* (BB-48), listing from torpedo hit, *Tennessee* (BB-43), *Oklahoma* (BB-37) alongside *Maryland* (BB-46), *Neosho* (AO-23), *California* (BB-44), off *Neosho's* port bow. Note smoke from Hickam Field, above left. (From a Japanese photograph taken during the attack.)
NH 50931

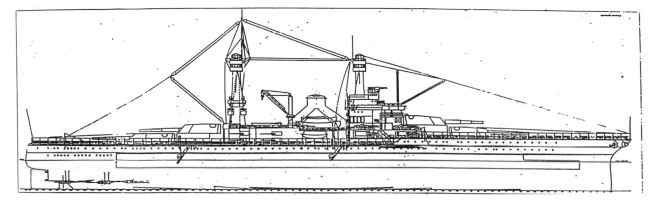

South Dakota outboard profile line drawing of *South Dakota* Class (BB-49–BB-54). Entire class cancelled and eventually scrapped in accordance with Washington Naval Treaty of Feb. 8, 1922. Taken from original ship's hull plan.   NATIONAL ARCHIVES MICROFILM ROLL 5958

1st Commanding Officer:

Authorized: August 29, 1916 and March 4, 1917

Keel Laid: March 15, 1920

Launched: No

Commissioned: Cancelled Feb. 8,1922

Sponsor:

Displacement Standard Tons: 41,400

Displacement Full Load Tons: 43,200

Design Crew Complement: 62 officers, 1129 enlisted

Main Guns: 12-16" 50 caliber (38,000-yard range with armor-piercing rounds)

Secondary Guns: 16-5"/53 caliber; 8-3"/50 caliber AA

Construction Costs: $15.5 million maximum plus armor and armament

Armor: Maximum thickness 18" at turret face plates

Length Overall: 660' waterline, 684' overall

Mean Draught: 33'

Extreme Beam: 106'

Torpedo Tubes: 2 21" submerged

Catapults: None

Builder: New York Navy Yard, Brooklyn, New York

Original Engines Manufactured: Turbines

Original Boilers Manufactured: Babcock & Wilcox type: WT

Original Fuel: Oil, 2100 tons (631,000 gallons)

Drive: Turbo-electric, 4 screws

Sisters: *South Dakota* Class of 1917

Designed Speed: 23 knots

Designed Shaft Horsepower: 60,000

Design Comments: Named ship of class of six 43,200-ton Battleships

History Highlights:

• Cancelled by Washington Naval Treaty of Feb. 8, 1922 when 38.5 percent complete; entire class was scrapped

Date Decommissioned: Unfinished hull sold for scrapping on the Slipway to Steel Scrap Corporation of Philadelphia

Commendations:

Final Disposition: Name struck from the Navy List on Nov. 10, 1923; scrapping completed on Nov. 15, 1924 in accordance with the Washington Naval Treaty

Indiana, artist's 1922 conception of BB-49 through BB-54, which were never completed. The artist was Rose Stokes.   NH 63502

1st Commanding Officer:

Authorized: August 29, 1916 and March 4, 1917

Keel Laid: Nov. 1, 1920

Launched: No

Commissioned: Cancelled Feb. 8, 1922

Sponsor:

Displacement Standard Tons: 41,400

Displacement Full Load Tons: 43,200

Design Crew Complement: 62 officers, 1129 enlisted

Main Guns: 12-16" 50 caliber (38,000-yard range with armor-piercing shells)

Secondary Guns: 16-6"/53 caliber; 8-3"/50 caliber AA

Construction Costs: $15.5 millions maximum plus armor and armament

Armor: Maximum thickness 18" at turret face plates

Length Overall: 660 ' waterline, 684' overall

Mean Draught: 33'

Extreme Beam: 106'

Torpedo Tubes: 2 21' submerged

Catapults: None

Builder: New York Navy Yard, Brooklyn, New York

Original Engines Manufactured: Turbines

Original Boilers Manufactured: Babcock & Wilcox type: WT

Original Fuel: Oil, 2100 tons (631,000 gallons)

Drive: Turbo-electric, 4 screws

Sisters: *South Dakota* Class of 1917

Designed Speed: 23 knots

Designed Shaft Horsepower: 60,000

Design Comments:

History Highlights:

• Cancelled by Washington Naval Treaty of Feb 8, 1922 when 34.7 percent complete; entire class was scrapped

Date Decommissioned:

Commendations:

Final Disposition: Name struck from the Navy List on August 24, 1923; scrapped in accordance with the Washington Naval Treaty on Oct. 25, 1923

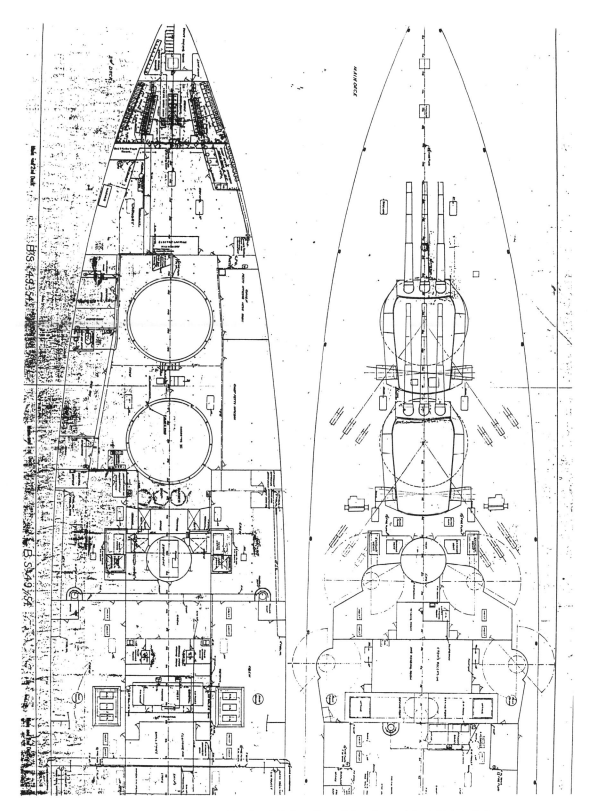

Indiana, main deck and second deck line drawings of the *South Dakota* Class. Taken from original ship's hull plans.

NATIONAL ARCHIVES MICROFILM ROLL 5958

1st Commanding Officer:

Authorized: August 29, 1916 and March 4, 1917

Keel Laid: Sept. 1, 1920

Launched: No

Commissioned: Cancelled Feb. 8, 1922

Sponsor:

Displacement Standard Tons: 41,400

Displacement Full Load Tons: 43,200

Design Crew Complement: 62 officers, 1129 enlisted

Main Guns: 12-16" 50 caliber (38,000-yard range with armor-peircing shells)

Secondary Guns: 16-6"/53 caliber; 8-3"/50 caliber AA

Construction Costs: $15.5 millions maximum plus armor and armament

Armor: Maximum thickness 18" at turret face plates

Length Overall: 660 ' waterline, 684' overall

Mean Draught: 33'

Extreme Beam: 106'

Torpedo Tubes: 2 21" submerged

Catapults: None

Builder: Mare Island Navy Yard, Vallejo, California

Original Engines Manufactured: Turbines

Original Boilers Manufactured: Babcock & Wilcox type: WT

Montana under construction at the Mare Island Navy Yard on Jan. 3, 1921. She was 27.6 percent complete when cancelled on Feb. 8, 1922. NH 74062

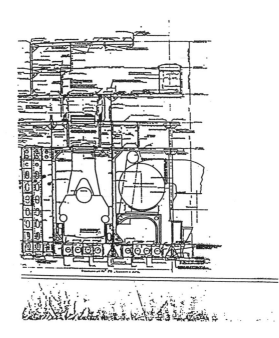

Montana, line drawing section at frame 78, looking aft. Taken from the ship's hull plans for Iowa (BB-53) of the South Dakota Class. NATIONAL ARCHIVES MICROFILM ROLL 5958

Original Fuel: Oil, 2100 tons (631,000 gallons)

Drive: Turbo-electric, 4 screws

Sisters: South Dakota Class of 1917

Designed Speed: 23 knots

Designed Shaft Horsepower: 60,000

Design Comments:

History Highlights:

· Cancelled by the Washington Naval Treaty of Feb 8, 1922 when 27.6 percent complete; entire class was scrapped

Date Decommissioned:

Commendations:

Final Disposition: Name struck from the Navy List on August 24, 1923; scrapped in accordance with the Washington Naval Treaty on Oct. 25, 1923

North Carolina art work by F. Muller, circa 1916–20. A slightly different view of the ships of this class had they been completed. *South Dakota* (BB-49), *Indiana* (BB-50), *Montana* (BB-51), *North Carolina* (BB-52), *Iowa* (BB-53) and *Massachusetts* (BB-54). All were cancelled under the Washington Naval Treaty of Feb 8, 1922. NH 44895

1st Commanding Officer:

Authorized: August 29, 1916–July 1, 1918–July 11, 1919

Keel Laid: Jan. 12, 1920

Launched: No

Commissioned: Cancelled Feb. 8, 1922

Sponsor:

Displacement Standard Tons: 41,400

Displacement Full Load Tons: 43,200

Design Crew Complement: 62 officers, 1129 enlisted

Main Guns: 12-16" 50 caliber (38,000-yard range with armor-piercing shells)

Secondary Guns: 16-6"/53 caliber; 8-3"/50 caliber AA

Construction Costs: $15.5 million maximum plus armor and armament

Armor: Maximum thickness 18" at turret face plates

Length Overall: 660' waterline, 684' overall

Mean Draught: 33'

Extreme Beam: 106'

Torpedo Tubes: 2 21" submerged

Catapults: None

Builder: Norfolk Navy Yard, Portsmouth, Virginia

Original Engines Manufactured: Turbines

Original Boilers Manufactured: Babcock & Wilcox type: WT

Original Fuel: Oil, 2100 tons (631,000 gallons)

Drive: Turbo-electric, 4 screws

Sisters: *South Dakota* Class of 1917

Designed Speed: 23 knots

Designed Shaft Horsepower: 60,000

Design Comments:

History Highlights:

· Cancelled by the Washington Naval Treaty of Feb. 8, 1922

when 36.7 percent complete; entire class was scrapped

Date Decommissioned:

Commendations:

Final Disposition: Name struck from the Navy List on Nov. 10, 1923; scrapped in accordance with the Washington Naval Treaty on Oct. 25, 1923

North Carolina, 16"/50 MK-2 model 1 gun barrel on display in East Willard Park, Washington Navy Yard, in October, 1974. This gun is serial #111, built in the Washington Navy Yard in 1922 and intended for use as the main battery armament in the *South Dakota* class (BB-49 through BB-54) and (CC-1) Class capital ships. Displayed alongside are two inert 16"/50 projectiles fired by *New Jersey* (BB-62) during shore bombardment practice in 1968. Note the railway car type mounting for the gun. NH 81482

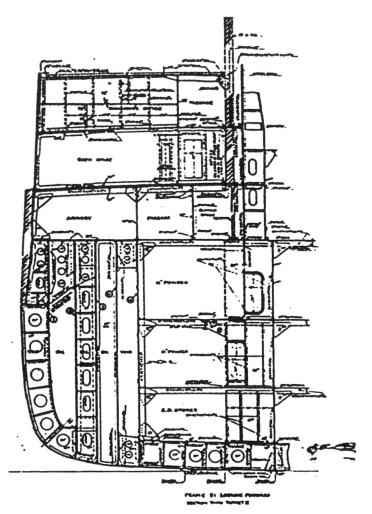

Above: *Iowa*, inboard profile line drawing of the *South Dakota* Class (BB-49 through BB-54) taken from the original ship's hull plans.

1st Commanding Officer:

Authorized: August 29, 1916–July 1, 1918–July 11, 1919

Keel Laid: May 17, 1920

Launched: No

Commissioned: Cancelled Feb. 8, 1922

Sponsor:

Displacement Standard Tons: 41,400

Displacement Full Load Tons: 43,200

Design Crew Complement: 62 officers, 1129 enlisted

Main Guns: 12-16" 50 caliber (38,000-yard range with armor-piercing rounds)

Secondary Guns: 16-6"/53 caliber; 8-3"/50 caliber AA

Construction Costs: $15.5 millions maximum plus armor and armament

Armor: Maximum thickness 18" at turret face plates

Length Overall: 660' waterline, 684' overall

Mean Draught: 33'

Extreme Beam: 106'

Torpedo Tubes: 2 21" submerged

Catapults: None

Builder: Newport News Shipbuilding Co., Newport News, Virginia

Original Engines Manufactured: Turbines

Original Boilers Manufactured: Babcock & Wilcox type: WT

Original Fuel: Oil, 2100 tons (631,000 gallons)

Drive: Turbo-electric, 4 screws

Sisters: *South Dakota* Class of 1917

Designed Speed: 23 knots

Designed Shaft Horsepower: 60,000

Design Comments:

History Highlights:

· Cancelled by the Washington Naval Treaty of Feb. 8, 1922 when 31.8 percent complete; entire class was scrapped

· Construction cancelled on August 17, 1923

Date Decommissioned:

Commendations:

Final Disposition: Name struck from the Navy List August 24, 1923; scrapped in accordance with the Washington Naval Treaty of Nov. 8, 1923

Iowa, line drawing at frame 51, looking forward sectioned through the turret, taken from *Iowa* (BB-53) hull plans for the class.

1st Commanding Officer:

Authorized: August 29, 1916–July 1, 1918–July 11, 1919

Keel Laid: April 4, 1921

Launched:

Commissioned: Cancelled Feb 8, 1922

Sponsor:

Displacement Standard Tons: 41,400

Displacement Full Load Tons: 43,200

Design Crew Complement: 62 officers, 1129 enlisted

Main Guns: 12-16" 50 caliber (38,000-yard range with armor-piercing rounds)

Secondary Guns: 16-6"/53 caliber; 8-3"/50 caliber AA

Construction Costs: $15.5 million maximum plus armor and armament

Armor: Maximum thickness 18" at turret face plates

Length Overall: 660' waterline, 684' overall

Mean Draught: 33'

Extreme Beam: 106'

Torpedo Tubes: 2 21" submerged

Catapults: None

Builder: Bethlehem Steel Co., Quincy, Massachusetts

Original Engines Manufactured: Turbines

Original Boilers Manufactured: Babcock & Wilcox type: WT

Original Fuel: Oil, 2100 tons (631,000 gallons)

Drive: Turbo-electric, 4 screws

Sisters: *South Dakota* Class of 1917

Designed Speed: 23 knots

Designed Shaft Horsepower: 60,000

Design Comments:

History Highlights:

· Cancelled by Washington Naval Treaty of Feb 8, 1922 when 11 percent complete; entire class scrapped

· Unfinished hull was sold for scrap on Nov. 8, 1923 to Steel Scrap Co. of Philadelphia

Date Decommissioned:

Commendations:

Final Disposition: Name struck from the Navy List on August 24, 1923; scrapped in accordance with Washington Naval Treaty on Nov. 8, 1923

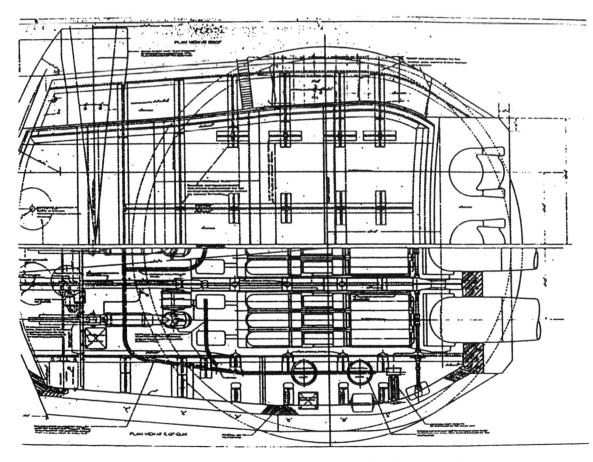

Massachusetts, line drawing plan view at roof (top center line) and plan view at center line of gun. Taken from original ship's hull plan. NATIONAL ARCHIVES MICROFILM ROLL 5958

North Carolina at sea in 1941 after her April 9 commissioning. (The first American fast battleship.)
NH 61327

1st Commanding Officer: Capt. O. M. Hustvedt

Authorized: March 27, 1934 and June 3, 1936

Keel Laid: Oct. 27, 1937

Launched: June 13, 1940

Commissioned: April 9, 1941

Sponsor: Miss Isabel Hoey

Displacement Standard Tons: 35,000 (increased to 36,600 by 1942)

Displacement Full Load Tons: 41,000 (increased to 44,800 by 1942)

Design Crew Complement: 108 officers, 1772 enlisted, 2500 for war service

Main Guns: 9-16" 45 caliber MK6 (40,600-yard range with armor-piercing rounds)

Secondary Guns: 20-5"/38 caliber MK 12; 4-Quad 1.1"; 12-.50 caliber (modifications with 60-40 millimeter/ 56 QUAD AA; 36-20 millimeter/70 (S) AA)

Construction Costs: $76,885,750

Armor: Maximum thickness 18" at turret face plates

Length Overall: 713'5" waterline, 728'9" overall

Mean Draught: 31'7" normal, 35'6" maximum

Extreme Beam: 108'4"

Torpedo Tubes: None

Catapults: 2-AFT

Builder: New York Navy Yard, Brooklyn, New York

Original Engines Manufactured: General Electric geared turbines

Original Boilers Manufactured: Babcock & Wilcox type: WT; no. 8

Original Fuel: Oil, 7167 tons (2,150,100 gallons)

Drive: Turbine, 4 screws

Sisters: *North Carolina* Class

Designed Speed: 28 knots

Designed Shaft Horsepower: 121,000

Design Comments: First-class Battleship; oil-fired boilers; the first commissioned of the U.S. Navy's modern fast battleships

History Highlights:

· Active December, 1941; to the Pacific Fleet on June 10, 1942; Guadalcanal and Tulagi on August 7, 1942; August 24, 1942 Battle of Eastern Solomons

· Sept. 15, 1942 torpedo hits port side killing 5; New Georgia group June 30 to August 31, 1943; Gilbert Islands Nov. 19 to Dec. 8, 1943

· Bismark Archipelago , Dec. 25, 1943; Marshall Islands Jan. 29 to Feb. 8, 1944; task force strikes on Truk Feb. 16 to May 1, 1944

· Western New Guinea, April 21–24, 1944; April 6, 1945 off Okinawa—a 5" friendly fire hit kills 3 and wounds 44

· Marianas invasion of Saipan June 11 to 24, 1944; Battle of the Philippine Sea June 19 and 20, 1944; Leyte operation Nov. 13–25, 1944 and Dec. 14–16, 1944

· Luzon Operation Jan. 6–22, 1945; Iwo Jima Feb. 15, 1945; raids on Honshu and Nansei Shoto from Feb. 15 to March 1, 1945

· Okinawa Invasion March 17–April 27, 1945; Third Fleet operations on Japanese Home Islands July 10– August 15, 1945

· Overhaul at New York late 1945, early 1946; 1946 summer training cruise for midshipmen

Date Decommissioned: 1947 inactivated; decommissioned at New York on June 27. 1947; struck on June 1, 1960; transferred to North Carolina on Sept. 6, 1961

Commendations: Fifteen WWII Battle Stars

Final Disposition: April 29, 1962 dedicated at Wilmington, North Carolina as a memorial to North Carolinans of all services killed in World War II.

North Carolina aerial port broadside view of memorial where she been berthed since April 29, 1962 in Wilmington, North Carolina.

COLLECTION OF BATTLESHIP *NORTH CAROLINA.* COURTESY BATTLESHIP *NORTH CAROLINA.*

North Carolina stern view of memorial proudly showing her namesake.

COLLECTION OF BATTLESHIP *NORTH CAROLINA.* COURTESY BATTLESHIP *NORTH CAROLINA*

USS Washington
BB-56

1st Commanding Officer: Capt. H. H. J. Benson
Authorized: March 27, 1934 and June 3, 1936
Keel Laid: June 14, 1938
Launched: June 1, 1940
Commissioned: May 15, 1941
Sponsor: Miss Virginia Marshall
Displacement Standard Tons: 35,000
Displacement Full Load Tons: 41,000
Design Crew Complement: 108 officers, 1772 enlisted, 2500 for war service
Main Guns: 9-16" 45 caliber MK6 (40,600-yard range with armor-piercing rounds)
Secondary Guns: 20-5"/38 caliber MK 12; 4-QUAD 1.1"; 12-.50 caliber (modifications with 60-40 millimeter/ 56 QUAD AA; 36-20 millimeter/70 (S) AA)
Construction Costs: $76,885,750
Armor: Maximum thickness 18" at turret face plates
Length Overall: 729'
Mean Draught: 26'8"
Extreme Beam: 108'
Torpedo Tubes: None
Catapults: 2, aft
Builder: Philadelphia Navy Yard, Philadelphia
Original Engines Manufactured: General Electric geared turbines
Original Boilers Manufactured: Babcock & Wilcox type: WT; no. 8
Original Fuel: Oil, 6583 tons (1,974,900 gallons)
Drive: Turbine, 4 screws
Sisters: *North Carolina* Class
Designed Speed: 28 knots
Designed Shaft Horsepower: 121,000

Design Comments: First-class Battleship; oil-fired boilers
History Highlights:

- 1941 Flagship Commander Battleship Division 6 Atlantic Fleet; March 27, 1942 Admiral Wilcox lost overboard in the Atlantic; March, 1942 to British Home Fleet
- August 23, 1942 to Pacific Fleet Battleship Division 6; Nov. 15, 1942 Battle of Savo Island; sunk Japanese Battleship *Kirishima*
- January–October, 1943 Pacific Fleet; November, 1943 Gilbert and Marshall Islands; January, 1944 New Hebrides
- Feb. 1, 1944 off Kwajalein, rammed the *Indiana* (BB-58); June, 1944 Saipan and Tinian
- June 19, 1944 Battle of the Philippine Sea; June, 1944 Marianas and Guam; August 1944 Admiralty Islands and Palaus
- October–November, 1944 Okinawa, Luzon, Hong Kong, Canton and Tokyo; February, 1945 Iwo Jima
- February–March, 1945 Japanese Home Islands; April, 1945 Okinawa
- June 6, 1945 to Puget Sound for refit; Oct. 6, 1945 to the Atlantic Fleet; Nov. 2, 1945 "Magic Carpet" duty

Date Decommissioned: Out of commission in reserve at New York on June 27, 1947
Commendations: Thirteen WWII Battle Stars; memorial with ship's artifacts including bell and wheel at Washington's state capital in Olympia
Final Disposition: Struck from the Navy list on June 1, 1960; May 24, 1961 sold for scrapping to Lipsett Division, Luria Brothers of New York City.

Washington in the Delaware River off the Philadelphia Navy Yard, May 29, 1941, 14 days after commissioning.
NH 92635

Washington, photo taken aboard *North Carolina* (BB-55) June 30, 1994 showing typical 16" shell storage on the American fast battleships, *North Carolina* (BB-55) through *Wisconsin* (BB-64).

Washington, photo taken aboard *North Carolina* (BB-55) 30 June 1994 showing typical 16" powder storage on the American fast battleships, *North Carolina* (BB-55) through *Wisconsin* (BB-64). Usually six bags of powder were used to fire the shell.

USS South Dakota
BB-57

1st Commanding Officer: Capt. T. L. Gatch
Authorized: March 27, 1934 and June 3, 1936
Keel Laid: July 5, 1939
Launched: June 7, 1941
Commissioned: March 20, 1942
Sponsor: Mrs. Harlan J. Bushfield
Displacement Standard Tons: 35,000
Displacement Full Load Tons: 42,000 (increased to 45,200 during WWII)
Design Crew Complement: 115 officers, 1678 enlisted, 2500 for war service
Main Guns: 9-16" 45 caliber MK 6 (40,600-yard range with armor-piercing rounds)
Secondary Guns: 16-5"/38 caliber MK 12; 7-QUAL 1.1"; 35-20 millimeter (modifications with 20-5"/38 MK 12; 15-40 millimeter MK 1 QUAD AA; 22-20 millimeter MK4 (S) AA; 8-20 millimeter MK4 (2)AA)
Construction Costs: $77 million
Armor: Maximum thickness 18" at turret face plates
Length Overall: 680
Mean Draught: 29'3"
Extreme Beam: 108-2"
Torpedo Tubes: None

Catapults: 2, aft
Builder: New York Shipbuilding Corporation, Camden, New Jersey
Original Engines Manufactured: General Electric geared turbines
Original Boilers Manufactured: Babcock & Wilcox type: WT; no. 8
Original Fuel: Oil, 6950 tons (2,085,000 gallons)
Drive: Turbine, 4 screws (Maximum propeller diameter 17'8")
Sisters: *South Dakota* Class
Designed Speed: 27 knots
Designed Shaft Horsepower: 130,000
Design Comments: First-class Battleship; oil-fired boilers
History Highlights:
· June 3–July 26, 1942 shakedown August 16, 1942 to Pacific; Sept. 6, 1942 extensive hull damage on reef in Lahai Passage
· Oct. 26 and 27, 1942 Battle of Santa Cruz Island; 500-pound bomb hit the #1 turret; Oct. 30, 1942 collision with *Mahan* (DD-364)
· Nov. 14 and 15, 1942 Battle of Guadacanal; heavy damage from 42 enemy hits while helping sink Japanese Battleship *Kirishima*

South Dakota being scrapped possibly in late 1962 or early 1963 after being stricken from the naval list on June 1, 1962.
NH 89295

South Dakota underway sometime during her World War II service. NH 67848

- February, 1943 with *Ranger* (CV-4) in the North Atlantic; with the British Home Fleet until August, 1943; to Pacific Battleship Divisions 8 and 9 in November, 1943
- November and December, 1943 at Marshall Islands; April, 1944 at New Guinea; June, July and August, 1944 at Truk, Caroline and Saipan
- June 19, 1944 at 1012 Battle of the Philippine Sea; bomb hit to main deck killed 24 and injured 27; October, 1944 off Formosa
- February, 1945 Iwo Jima; February, 1945 Tokyo Fleet raids; March, 1945 Okinawa; May 6, 1945 #2 turret fire killed 8 and injured 24; July, 1945 Tokyo bombardment
- August 15, 1945 at Tokyo, the last strike of WWII; Japan capitulated that day; Sept. 2, 1945 in Tokyo Bay to witness the signing of the Japanese surrender

Date Decommissioned: June, 1946 with the Atlantic Reserve Fleet; Jan. 31, 1947 in reserve, out of commission

Commendations: Thirteen WWII Battle Stars; WWII Navy Unit Commendation; WWII Navy Occupation Service Medal; World War II Victory Medal; Philippine Liberation Medal; Philippine Republic Presidential unit Citation

Final Disposition: Struck from the Navy List on June 1, 1962; sold for scrapping to Lipsett Division, Luria Brothers, New York City; memorial dedicated on Sept. 7, 1969 in Sioux Falls, South Dakota

South Dakota, photo taken aboard North Carolina (BB-55) on June 30, 1994 showing the 16"
rifle looking forward from the starboard side typical on the American fast battleships, *North
Carolina* (BB-55) through *Wisconsin* (BB-64). The rifle barrel is approximately 60 feet long and
48 inches in outside diameter at its base. When the powder ignites internal pressure of
approximately 50,000 pounds per square inch is developed to expel the shell.

PERSONAL COLLECTION OF AUTHOR

South Dakota Memorial, port (bow left photo and starboard (bow) right photo showing the
main mast, 16-inch gun turret replicas, anchor chain and other parts of "USS *South
Dakota*" stand in place in a full-size layout of the main deck. The monument was built as a
memorial "To the memory of a great ship and the men who served aboard her, the
battleship 'X,' during World War II." The memorial is maintained by the USS South Dakota
Memorial Foundation in Sioux Falls, South Dakota.
PHOTO © COURTESY USS SOUTH DAKOTA MEMORIAL FOUNDATION

Inset: Indiana, bow view taken during her World War II service.
NATIONAL ARCHIVES PHOTOGRAPH 80-G-12195

Bottom: Indiana, being dismantled at the Nikolai Joffe Shipyard, Richmond, California on Nov. 22, 1963. NH 89294

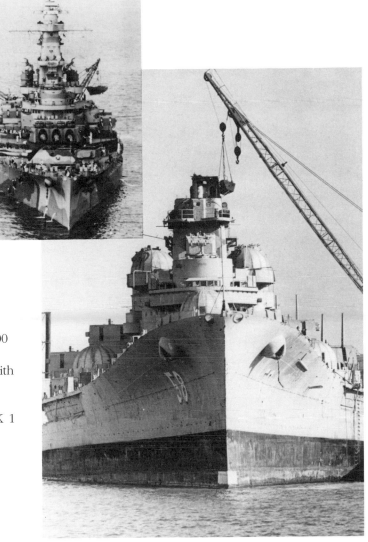

1st Commanding Officer: Capt. A. S. Merrill

Authorized: March 27, 1934 and June 3, 1936

Keel Laid: Nov. 20, 1939

Launched: Nov. 21, 1941

Commissioned: April 30, 1942

Sponsor: Mrs. Lewis C. Robbins

Displacement Standard Tons: 35,000

Displacement Full Load Tons: 42,000

Design Crew Complement: 115 officers, 1678 enlisted, 2500 for war service

Main Guns: 9-16" 45 caliber MK6 (40,600-yard range with armor-piercing rounds)

Secondary Guns: 20-5"/38 caliber MK 12; 6-QUAD 40 millimeter; (modification with 15-40 millimeter MK 1 QUAD AA; 22-20 millimeter (S) MK 4 AA; 8-20 millimeter (2) MK4 AA)

Construction Costs: $77 million

Armor: Maximum thickness 18" at turret face plates

Length Overall: 680'

Mean Draught: 29'3"

Extreme Beam: 108-2"

Torpedo Tubes: none

Catapults: 2, aft

Builder: Newport News Shipbuilding Co., Newport News, Virginia

Original Engines Manufactured: Westinghouse geared turbines

Original Boilers Manufactured: Foster-Wheeler WT; no. 8

Original Fuel: Oil, 7340 tons (2,202,000 gallons)

Drive: Turbine, 4 screws (maximum propeller diameter 17'8")

Sisters: *South Dakota* Class

Designed Speed: 27 knots

Designed Shaft Horsepower: 130,000

Design Comments: First-class Battleship, oil-fired boilers

History Highlights:

• June, 1942 to Pacific Fleet; Nov. 28, 1942 with Admiral Lee's carrier force *Enterprise* (CV-6) and *Sarasota* (CV-3)

• Oct. 21, 1943 at Pearl Harbor; Nov. 11, 1943 Gilbert Islands; January, 1944 at Kwajalein

• Feb. 1, 1944 collided with *Washington* (BB-56); damage to starboard side; April 29 and 30, 1944 with Task Force 58 and at Truk

• June 19, 1944 Battle of the Philippine Sea "Marianas Turkey Shoot"; August–September, 1944 preparing for the invasion of Leyte

• January and February, 1945 Iwo Jima; March, 1945 Okinawa and carrier support; June 13, 1945 in San Pedro Bay, Philippines

• July 1 to August 15, 1945 Task Group 38.1 bombarded Japanese Home Islands and supported carrier air strikes

Sept. 5, 1945 to Sept. 14, 1945 in Tokyo Bay; Sept. 29, 1945 to San Francisco; in reserve in commission at Bremerton Sept. 11, 1946

Date Decommissioned: Sept. 11, 1947 in Pacific Reserve Fleet

Commendations: Nine WWII Battle Stars

Final Disposition: Stricken on June 1, 1962; sold for scrap. Her mast is at the University of Indiana and her anchor is at Fort Wayne, Indiana; other items are in various state museums

Massachusetts, in Puget Sound, Washington, on Jan. 22, 1945. NH 46430

1st Commanding Officer: Capt. F. E. M. Whiting

Authorized: March 27, 1934 and June 3, 1936

Keel Laid: July 20, 1939

Launched: Sept. 23, 1941

Commissioned: May 12, 1942

Sponsor: Mrs. Charles Francis Adams

Displacement Standard Tons: 35,000 (modified to 35,113 by 1946)

Displacement Full Load Tons: 42,000 (modified to 45.216 by 1946)

Design Crew Complement: 115 officers, 1678 enlisted, 2500 for war service

Main Guns: 9-16" 45 caliber MK 6 (40,600-yard range with armor-piercing rounds)

Secondary Guns: 20-5"/38 caliber MK 12; 6-QUAD 40 millimeter; (modifications with 15-40 millimeter 1 QUAD AA; 22-20 millimeter (S) MK4 AA; 8-20 millimeter (2) MK 4 AA)

Construction Costs: $77 million

Armor: Maximum thickness 18" at turret face plates

Length Overall: 680'10"

Mean Draught: 29'3"

Extreme Beam: 107'11"

Torpedo Tubes: None

Catapults: 2, aft

Builder: Bethlehem Steel Co., Quincy, Massachusetts

Original Engines Manufactured: General Electric geared turbines

Original Boilers Manufactured: Babcock & Wilcox type: WT; no. 8

Original Fuel: Oil, 6950 tons (2,085,000 gallons)

Drive: Turbine, 4 screws (maximum propeller diameter 17'8")

Sisters: *South Dakota* Class

Designed Speed: 27 knots

Designed Shaft Horsepower: 130,000

Design Comments: First-class Battleship; oil-fired boilers

History Highlights:
- Nov. 8, 1942 invasion of North Africa at 0740 hours; in battle with the French Battleship *Jean Bart*, she silenced the French Battleship's 15" guns
- March 4, 1943 to the Pacific Fleet; Nov. 19, 1943 to Feb. 8, 1944 Gilbert Islands
- Jan. 29 to Feb 8, 1944 Marshall Islands, Kwajalein and Majuro Atolls; Feb. 16 and 17, 1944 Truk
- Feb. 11 to 22, 1944 Marianas; March 30 to April 1, 1944 Palau, Yap, Ulithi; April 29 to May 1, 1944 Truk, Satawan and Ponape
- April 21–24, 1944 Hollandia Operation; Sept. 6 to Oct 14, 1944 Western Caroline Islands; Oct. 10, 1944 Leyte Operation, and Okinawa
- Oct. 22–27, 1944 Battle of Leyte Gulf with Task Group 38.3; December, 1944 invasion of Mindoro
- January, 1945 at landing of Lingayen; February and March, 1945 at Iwo Jima; Feb. 15 to March 1, 1945 Honshu and Nansei Shoto, Japan
- Okinawa operation March 17 to June 11, 1945; Third Fleet raids on Japanese Home Islands July 10 to August 15, 1945; August 9, 1945 at Kamaishi, Japan she fired the last 16" shell of WWII

Date Decommissioned: March 27, 1947 Atlantic Reserve Fleet; struck from the Navy List on June 1, 1962

Commendations: Eleven WWII Battle Stars; Philippine Republic Presidential Unit Citation

Final Disposition: June 4, 1965 to Massachusetts as a memorial to all war veterans of the Commonwealth; August 14, 1965 enshrined at Fall River, Massachusetts

Massachusetts, aerial starboard broadside (left), and starboard broadside (bottom) views of the ship, along with the destoyer *Joseph P. Kennedy Jr.* (DD-850), submarine *Lionfish (*SS-298), PT Boats 617 and 796, a landing craft, mechanized (LCM), and a section of the bow of the heavy cruiser *Fall River* (CA-131), at the memorial berth in Fall River, Massachusetts. *Massachusetts* has been a memorial since her dedication ceremonies on August 14, 1965.

1st Commanding Officer: Capt. G. B. Wilson

Authorized: March 27, 1934 and June 3, 1936

Keel Laid: Feb 1, 1940

Launched: Feb. 16, 1942

Commissioned: August 16, 1942

Sponsor: Mrs. Lister Hill

Displacement Standard Tons: 35,000

Displacement Full Load Tons: 42,000 (modified to 43,000 by 1946)

Design Crew Complement: 115 officers, 1678 enlisted, 2500 for war service

Main Guns: 9-16" 45 caliber MK 6 (40,600-yard range with armor-piercing rounds)AP)

Secondary Guns: 20-5"/MK 12; 6 QUAD 40 millimeter (modifications with 12-40 millimeter MK 1 QUAD AA; 52-20 millimeter (S) MK4 AA; 8-20 millimeter (2) MK4 AA)

Construction Costs: $77 million

Armor: Maximum thickness 18" at turret face plates

Length Overall: 680'

Mean Draught: 29'3"

Extreme Beam: 108-2"

Torpedo Tubes: None

Catapults: 2, aft

Builder: Norfolk Navy Yard, Portsmouth, Virginia

Original Engines Manufactured: Westinghouse geared turbines

Original Boilers Manufactured: Foster-Wheeler WT; no. 8

Original Fuel: Oil, 7340 tons (2,202,000 gallons)

Drive: Turbine, 4 screws (maximum propeller diameter 17'8")

Sisters: *South Dakota* Class

Designed Speed: 27 knots

Designed Shaft Horsepower: 130,000

Design Comments: First-class Battleship; oil-fired boilers

Inset: *Alabama* as a memorial at her birth off Interstate 10 in Mobile, Alabama. She has been a memorial since Jan. 9, 1965 and is open every day except Christmas. Photo circa 1994.

COURTESY USS *ALABAMA* BATTLESHIP COMMISSION

Left: A*labama* anchored in Casco Bay, Maine, in December, 1942 or January, 1943, six months after commissioning. Preparing for her combat service.

NATIONAL ARCHIVES PHOTOGRAPH 80-G-37943

Left: *Alabama* in March, 1945 wearing Measure 22 camouflage (hull blue, superstructure gray) she wore for most of her combat service. Also showing the full array of armament she wore at the end of her World War II service.

NATIONAL ARCHIVES PHOTOGRAPH 80-G-31680, COURTESY USS *ALABAMA* BATTLESHIP COMMISSION

Alabama, circa November, 1942, showing Measure 12 (dapple) camouflage, she wore from her August, 1942 commissioning until just prior to her Atlantic and North Sea combat service.

NATIONAL ARCHIVES PHOTOGRAPH, 80-G-31558 COURTESY USS *ALABAMA* BATTLESHIP COMMISSION

History Highlights:
· September, 1942 with the Atlantic Fleet operating with the British Home Fleet protecting convoys to Britain and Russia
· August, 1943 to the Pacific Fleet 3rd Fleet at Efate, New Hebrides
· Joined fast carrier forces in October, 1943 providing fire support and anti-aircraft screening
· Gilbert Islands Nov. 19 to Dec. 8, 1943; Kwajalein and Majuro from Jan. 29 to Feb 8, 1944; Truk, Feb. 16 and 17, 1944
· Marianas Feb. 21 and 22, 1944; Hollandia landings April 21 to 24, 1944; invasion of Saipan June 11 to 24, 1944
· Battle of the Philippine Sea June 19 and 20, 1944; invasion of Guam July 12 to August 15, 1944; Philippine Islands raids Sept. 6 to Oct. 12, 1944

· Okinawa raid on Oct. 10, 1944; Luzon and Formosa raids Oct. 10 to 12, 1944; battle for Leyte Gulf Oct. 25 and 26, 1944
· Invasion of Okinawa May 9 to June 11, 1945; Third Fleet raids on Japanese Home Islands July 10 to August 15, 1945; support the occupation of Tokyo from Sept. 5 to 20, 1945

Date Decommissioned: To San Francisco in September, 1945; out of commission in reserve on Jan. 9 , 1947; stricken from the Navy List on June 1, 1962

Commendations: Nine WWII Battle Stars; Navy Occupation Service Medal; Pacific Philippine Republic Presidential Unit Citation Badge

Final Disposition: Serving as a memorial at Mobile, Alabama since she was dedicated on Jan. 9, 1965 to the men and women of Alabama who served in WWII and Korea

1st Commanding Officer: Capt. J. L. McCrea

Authorized: March 27, 1934–June 3, 1936–May 17, 1938

Keel Laid: June 27, 1940

Launched: August 27, 1942

Commissioned: Feb. 22, 1943

Sponsor: Mrs. Henry A. Wallace

Displacement Standard Tons: 45,000

Displacement Full Load Tons: 57,600 (modified to 58,000 when recommissioned in 1986)

Design Crew Complement: 117 officers, 1804 enlisted, 2700 for war service WWII

Main Guns: 9-16"/50 caliber MK 7 (41,600-yard range with armor-piercing rounds)

Secondary Guns: 20-5" 38 caliber; 15-QUAD 40 millimeter; 60-20 millimeter (modernizations of the 80s: 8-MK 143 Tomahawk ABLSs 4-MK 141 Harpoon; 6-MK 38 5"/38 (2); 4-MK 15 CIWS)

Construction Costs: $100 million (80s reactivatation $496 million)

Armor: Maximum thickness 18" at turret face plates

Length Overall: 887'7"

Mean Draught: 28'11"

Extreme Beam: 108'2"

Torpedo Tubes: None

Catapults: 2, aft (modernization with 80s helicopter pad)

Builder: New York Navy Yard, Brooklyn, New York

Original Engines Manufactured: General Electric geared turbines

Original Boilers Manufactured: Babcock & Wilcox type; WT; no. 8

Original Fuel: Oil, 7073 tons (2,121,900 gallons)

Drive: Turbine, 4 screws (maximum propeller diameter 18'3")

Sisters: *Iowa* Class

Designed Speed: 33 knots

Designed Shaft Horsepower: 212,000

Design Comments: First-class Battleship; oil-fired boilers

History Highlights:

- August 27, 1943 to Newfoundland to neutralize the threat of German Battleship *Tirpitz*
- Fall of 1943 carried Franklin Delano Roosevelt to and from the Teheran Conference
- Jan. 2, 1944 to Pacific as Flagship Battleship Division 7; January, 1944 Marshalls, Kwajalein, Eniwetok, Truk
- March 18, 1944 hit by two Japanese 4.7" shells; April, 1944 New Guinea and the Carolines
- June 19, 1944 Battle of the Philippine Sea; October, 1944 Battle for Leyte Gulf; March, 1945 Okinawa
- May 6–8, 1945 off Japanese Home Islands; August 29, 1945 to Sept. 20, 1945 in Tokyo Bay as Admiral Halsey's Flagship
- April 8 to Oct. 16, 1952 off Korea; Jan. 4, 1957 with the 6th Fleet in the Mediterranean
- Recommissioned April 28, 1984 to serve in Carrier and Battleship Command and Support Groups, also as a Command and Control ship; April 19, 1989, turret explosion in the #2 turret killed 47

Date Decommissioned: Commissioned Feb. 22, 1943, decommissioned March 24, 1949; recommissioned August 25, 1951, decommissioned Feb. 24, 1958; recommissioned April 28, 1984, decommissioned Oct. 26, 1990

Commendations: Nine WWII Battle Stars, two Korean Battle Stars; United Nations Service Medal; Korean Service Medal; Korean and Philippine Presidential Unit Citations and others

Final Disposition: 1990 Reserve Fleet at Philadelphia Navy Yard; stricken from the Navy list January 12, 1995, awaiting final disposition

Iowa (BB-61) and *Wisconsin* (BB-64), starboard bow view, in the Atlantic Reserve Fleet at the Philadelphia Navy Yard on Oct. 30, 1994.

PERSONAL COLLECTION OF AUTHOR

1st Commanding Officer: Capt. C. F. Holden
Authorized: March 27, 1934–June 3, 1936–May 17, 1938
Keel Laid: Sept. 16, 1940
Launched: Dec. 7, 1942
Commissioned: May 23, 1943
Sponsor: Mrs. Charles Edison
Displacement Standard Tons: 45,000
Displacement Full Load Tons: 57,600 (modernized to 58,000 when recommissioned in 1982)
Design Crew Complement: 117 officers, 1804 enlisted, 2700 for war service WWII
Main Guns: 9-16"/50 caliber MK 7 (41,600-yard range with armor-piercing rounds)
Secondary Guns: 20-5" 38 caliber 15-QUAD 40 millimeter; 60-20 millimeter (1980s modernization of the 80s: 8-MK 143 Tomahawk ABL'S 40MK 141 Harpoon 6-MK 38 caliber 5"/38 (2) 4-MK 15 CIWS)
Construction Costs: $100 million (1980s reactivation $496 million)
Armor: Maximum thickness 18" at turret face plates
Length Overall: 887'7"
Mean Draught: 28'11"
Extreme Beam: 108'1"
Torpedo Tubes: None
Catapults: 2, aft (1968 modernized with helicopter pad)
Builder: Philadelphia Navy Yard
Original Engines Manufactured: Westinghouse geared turbines
Original Boilers Manufactured: Babcock & Wilcox type; W'T; no. 8
Original Fuel: Oil, 7251 tons (2,175,300 gallons)
Drive: Turbine, 4 screws (maximum prop diameter 18'3")
Sisters: *Iowa* Class
Designed Speed: 33 knots
Designed Shaft Horsepower: 212,000
Design Comments: First-class Battleship, oil-fired boilers
History Highlights:
- Jan. 29–Feb. 2, 1944 Kwajalein and Eniwetok Islands; April 13–May 4, 1944 New Guinea; April 29–30, 1944 Truk; June 19, 1944 Battle of the Philippine Sea
- August 9, 1944 Flagship Third Fleet with Admiral Halsey at Okinawa, Formosa, Visayas, Leyte and Cebu
- Oct. 29, 1944 friendly fire from *Intrepid* (CV-11) 3 on *New Jersey* were wounded; Dec. 30, 1944–Jan. 25, 1945 Formosa, Okinawa, Luzon
- Feb. 19–21, 1945 at Iwo Jima; March 14–April 16, 1946 at Okinawa; Sept. 17, 1945–Jan. 28, 1946 in Tokyo Bay as Flagship
- May 20, 1951 first shelling of Korea at Wonsan; April, 12, 1953 bombarded Congjin, Korea; May 26, 1953 last shelling of Korea at Wonsan
- Sept. 30, 1968 near 17th parallel first shelling in Viet-

New Jersey, photo taken Jan. 17, 1991 in the Persian Gulf aboard battleship *Missouri* (BB-63) on the first day of Operation Desert Storm offensive against Iraq. A Tomahawk BGM-109 land attack missile (TLAM) is fired from a Mark 143 launcher. A Phalanx Mark 15 close-in weapons system (CIWS) stands in the foreground. These weapons are typical of the four *Iowa* class ships following their 1980s upgrades and recommissions.

DOD STILL MEDIA RECORDS CENTER PHOTOGRAPH   DN-SN-91-08058

nam at the Demilitarized Zone (DMZ), with 6 months of shelling to follow
- Recommissioned Dec. 28, 1982 to serve in Carrier and Battleship Command and Support groups, also as a Command and Control ship

Date Decommissioned: Commissioned May 23, 1943, decommissioned June 30, 1948; recommissioned Nov. 21, 1950, decommissioned August 21, 1957; recommissioned April 6, 1968, decommissioned Dec. 17, 1969; recommissioned Dec. 28, 1982, decommissioned Feb. 8, 1991
Commendations: Nine WWII battle Stars, four Korean Battle Stars; Navy Unit Citation for Vietnam
Final Disposition: 1992 Reserve Fleet at Bremerton, Washington; stricken from the Navy list January 12, 1995, awaiting final disposition

New Jersey off the Philadelphia Navy Yard, circa May, 1943, several days following her May 23 commissioning. Note the paravane chain at her bow and the absence of the usual *Iowa* Class bow bulwark, yet to be installed.
NH 92293

Missouri (BB-63) is shown firing her forward 16" main batteries during World War II. Note the six 16" shells in the air. (She is the last American fast battleship to be commissioned, and the last American battleship to be completed.)
NH 58157

1st Commanding Officer: Capt. W. M. Callaghan

Authorized: March 27, 1934–June 3, 1936–May 17, 1938

Keel Laid: Jan. 6, 1941

Launched: Jan. 29, 1944

Commissioned: June 11, 1944

Sponsor: Miss Margaret Truman

Displacement Standard Tons: 45,000

Displacement Full Load Tons: 57,600 (modified to 58,000 when recommissioned in 1986)

Design Crew Complement: 117 officers, 1804 enlisted, 2700 for war service WWII

Main Guns: 9-16"/50 caliber MK 7 (41,600-yard range with armor-piercing rounds)

Secondary Guns: 20-5" 38 caliber 15-QUAD 40 millimeter; 60-20 millimeter (1980s modernized with 8-MK 143 Tomahawk ABLs 40MK 141 Harpoon 6-MK 38 caliber 5"/38 caliber (2) 4-MK 15 CIWS)

Construction Costs: $100 million (1980s reactivation $496 million)

Armor: Maximum thickness 18" at turret face plates

Length Overall: 887'3"

Mean Draught: 28'11"

Extreme Beam: 108'2"

Torpedo Tubes: None

Catapults: 2, aft (1980s modernized with helicopter pad)

Builder: New York Navy Yard, Brooklyn, New York

Original Engines Manufactured: General Electric geared turbines

Original Boilers Manufactured: Babcock & Wilcox type: WT; no. 8

Original Fuel: Oil, 7251 tons (2,175,000 gallons)

Drive: Turbine, 4 screws (maximum prop diameter 18'3")

Sisters: *Iowa* Class

Designed Speed: 33 knots

Designed Shaft Horsepower: 212,000

Design Comments: First-class Battleship; oil-fired boilers; last Battleship completed by the United States

History Highlights:

- Jan. 13, 1945 at West Caroline Islands; Feb. 16, 1945 with Task Force 58 and with the first air strikes on Japan since the Doolittle Raid of April, 1942
- Feb. 19, 1945 invasion of Iwo Jima; March 14, 1945 with carrier raids on Japan; April 1, 1945 at Okinawa
- Was in carrier group that sank Japanese Battleship *Yamato* on April 7, 1945, which had the world's largest guns at 18.2"
- April 11, 1945 hit by kamikaze near the main deck; July and August 1945 with carrier raids on the Japanese Home Islands
- Sept. 2, 1945 the Japanese formal surrender for WWII took place on her on deck from 0902 to 0930 hours; March 25, 1949 only U.S. Battleship in commission
- Jan 17, 1950 when 1.6 miles from Thimble Shoals Light she ran aground; refloated on Feb. 1, 1950
- Sept 14–March 19, 1951 Korea; Oct. 25, 1952–Jan. 2, 1953 Korea; Feb. 1, 1953–March 25, 1953 Korea
- Recommissioned July 1, 1986 to serve in Carrier and Battleship Command and Support groups, and as a Command and Control ship; served in Operation Desert Storm from Jan. 15 to Feb. 27, 1991

Date Decommissioned: Commissioned June 11, 1944, decommissioned Feb 26, 1955; recommissioned July 1, 1986, decommissioned March 31, 1992

Commendations: Three WWII Battle Stars, five for Korea; served in Operation Desert Storm

Final Disposition: 1992 Reserve Fleet at Bremerton, Washington; a plate in her deck marks the spot of the signing of the Japanese Surrender Papers on Sept. 2, 1945 ending World War II; stricken from the Navy list January 12, 1995, awaiting final disposition

Missouri, photo taken Jan. 12, 1991 in the Persian Gulf. An Iraqi mine floats near the *Missouri* prior to being detonated by explosive ordnance disposal (EOD) team members during Operation Desert Shield. Note the helicopter on the helipad in place of the earlier crane, catapults and spotting planes.

DOD STILL MEDIA RECORDS CENTER PHOTOGRAPH DN-SN-91-08060

1st Commanding Officer: Capt. E. E. Stone

Authorized: March 27, 1934–June 3, 1936–May 17, 1938

Keel Laid: Jan. 25, 1941

Launched: Dec. 7, 1943

Commissioned: April 16, 1944

Sponsor: Miss Walter S. Goodland

Displacement Standard Tons: 45,000

Displacement Full Load Tons: 57,600 (modified to 58,000 when recommissioned in 1987)

Design Crew Complement: 117 officers, 1804 enlisted, 2700 for war service

Main Guns: 9-16"/50 caliber MK 7 (41,600-yard range with armor-piercing rounds)

Secondary Guns: 20-5" 38 caliber 15-QUAD 40 millimeter; 60-20 millimeter (1980s modernized with 8-MK 143 Tomahawk ABL'S 40MK 141 Harpoon 6-MK 38 5"/ 38 caliber (2) 4-MK 15 CIWS)

Construction Costs: $100 million (1980s reactivation $496 million)

Armor: Maximum thickness 18" at turret face plates

Length Overall: 887'3"

Mean Draught: 28'11"

Extreme Beam: 108'3"

Torpedo Tubes: None

Catapults: 2, aft (1980s helicopter pad)

Builder: Philadelphia Navy Yard

Original Engines Manufactured: Westinghouse geared turbines

Original Boilers Manufactured: Babcock & Wilcox type: WT; no. 8

Original Fuel: Oil, 7251 tons (2,175,000 gallons)

Drive: Turbine, 4 screws (maximum propeller diameter 18'3")

Sisters: *Iowa* Class

Designed Speed: 33 knots

Designed Shaft Horsepower: 212,000

Design Comments: First-class Battleship; oil-fired boilers

History Highlights:

- Dec. 9, 1944 with Admiral Halsey's Third Fleet; Jan. 3–22, 1945 Lingayen Gulf Operations; January, 1945 in the South China Sea area
- February, 1945 at Iwo Jima, March, 1945 at Okinawa; March, 1945 at Japanese Home Islands; April, 1945 at Japanese Home Islands; June, 1945, also at Home Islands
- March 24, 1945 at Okinawa; July 8, 1945 Japanese Home Islands; Sept. 5, 1945 Tokyo Bay with Occupation forces; September, 1945 Magic Carpet Duty
- 1946/1947 Atlantic Fleet cruises; January, 1948 Atlantic Reserve Fleet
- Dec. 3, 1951 first shelling of Kasong, Korea; March 15, 1952 hit by 155 millimeter shell on the starboard 40 millimeter mount wounding 3 men; 1953–54 Atlantic Fleet training cruises

Wisconsin entering the Golden Gate, San Francisco, California, September, 1945 after the Japanese surrender in Tokyo Bay on Sept. 2. Note the World War II homeward-bound pennant. NH 66295

- May 6, 1955 collision with *Eaton* (DDE-510)—bow from *Kentucky* (BB-66) used for repair
- 1956-57 Atlantic, Mediterranean, Caribbean, and South Pacific cruises
- Recommissioned October 22, 1988, to serve in Carrier and Battleship Command and Support groups, and as a Command and Control ship; served in Operation Desert Storm from Jan 15 to Feb 27, 1991

Date Decommissioned: Commissioned April 16, 1944, decommissioned July 1, 1948; recommissioned March 3, 1951, decommissioned March 8, 1958; recommissioned October 22, 1988, decommissioned September 30, 1991

Commendations: Five WWII Battle Stars; one for Korea; served in Operation Desert Storm

Final Disposition: 1991 Reserve Fleet at Philadelphia Navy Yard; stricken from the Navy list January 12, 1995, awaiting final disposition

Wisconsin (BB-64) moored outboard of the hulk of *Oklahoma* (BB-37), at the Pearl Harbor Navy Yard on Nov. 11, 1944. Note the difference in length and beam of *Oklahoma* at 583 feet. And 95 feet to *Wisconsin* at 887 feet and 108 feet. The difference in construction dates is 1916 to 1944.
NH 78940

Wisconsin (BB-64) and *Iowa* (BB-61) in the Atlantic Reserve Fleet, starboard stern view at the Philadelphia Navy Yard on Oct. 30, 1994. PERSONAL COLLECTION OF AUTHOR

Illinois, Iowa (BB-62) photographed in 1943 shortly after her Feb. 22 commissioning. This photograph shows how the *Illinois* (BB-65) would have looked had she been completed in the same configuration as her sisters.
NH 53266

1st Commanding Officer:

Authorized: July 19, 1940

Keel Laid: Jan. 15, 1945

Launched: No

Commissioned: Cancelled August 12, 1945

Sponsor:

Displacement Standard Tons: 57,600

Displacement Full Load Tons: 57,600

Design Crew Complement: 117 officers, 1804 enlisted, 2700 for war service

Main Guns: 9-16"/50 caliber MK 7 (41,600-yard range with armor-piercing rounds)

Secondary Guns:

Construction Costs: $100 million

Armor: Maximum thickness 18" at turret face plates

Length Overall: 887'

Mean Draught: 28'11"

Extreme Beam: 108'

Torpedo Tubes: None

Catapults: 2, aft

Builder: Philadelphia Navy Yard

Original Engines Manufactured: Geared turbine

Original Boilers Manufactured: Babcock & Wilcox type

Original Fuel: Oil, 7251 tons (2,175,300 gallons)

Drive: Turbine, 4 screws (maximum propeller diameter 18'3")

Sisters: *Iowa* Class

Designed Speed: 33 knots

Designed Shaft Horsepower:

Design Comments: Construction cancelled on August 12, 1945

History Highlights:

· Cancelled on August 12, 1945 when 25 percent completed

Date Decommissioned:

Commendations: None

Final Disposition: Scraped, hull broken in place

USS Kentucky
BB-66

Kentucky, photo taken on Jan. 14, 1991 in the Persian Gulf. The fast combat support ship *Sacramento* (AOE-1), center, conducts an underway replenishment with the *Wisconsin* (BB-64), foreground, and the *Missouri* (BB-63) during Operation Desert Shield. Interestingly enough, *Sacramento* was originally built using one of the engine plants from *Kentucky*. The other plant went to *Sacramento's* sister ship *Camden* (AOE-2).

DOD STILL MEDIA RECORDS CENTER
PHOTOGRAPH DN-SN-91-09308

1st Commanding Officer:

Authorized: July 19, 1940

Keel Laid: Dec. 6, 1944

Launched: Jan. 20, 1950

Commissioned: Suspended Feb. 17, 1947

Sponsor:

Displacement Standard Tons: 45,000

Displacement Full Load Tons: 57,600

Design Crew Complement: 117 officers, 1804 enlisted, 2700 for war service

Main Guns: 9-16"/50 caliber MK 7 (41,600-yard range with armor-piercing rounds)

Secondary Guns:

Construction Costs: $100 million

Armor: Maximum thickness 18" at turret face plates

Length Overall: 887'

Mean Draught: 28'11"

Extreme Beam: 108'

Torpedo Tubes: None

Catapults: 2, aft

Builder: Norfolk Navy Yard, Norfolk, Virginia

Original Engines Manufactured: Geared turbine

Original Boilers Manufactured: Babcock & Wilcox type

Original Fuel: Oil, 7251 tons (2,175,300 gallons)

Drive: Turbine, 4 screws (maximum propellor diameter 18'3")

Sisters: *Iowa* Class

Designed Speed: 33 knots

Designed Shaft Horsepower:

Design Comments: Sold for scrap on Oct. 31, 1958

History Highlights:

• Construction suspended on Feb. 17, 1947 when 72.1 percent complete

• Designated SCB-19 in December, 1945

• The 120-ton, 68-foot-long section of her bow was used to repair the *Wisconsin* (BB-64) after she collided with the *Eaton* (DDE-510) on May 6, 1955

Date Decommissioned: Struck from Navy list on June 9, 1958

Commendations: None

Final Disposition: Sold for scrap to Boston Metals Co. of Baltimore, Maryland on Oct. 31, 1958

Kentucky shown at the Norfolk Naval Shipyard on Oct. 24, 1956. Her hull is 72 percent complete to the second deck (one deck below the weather deck) and is missing its bow, which was used to repair *Wisconsin* (BB-64) earlier in 1956. The bow section on her deck forward may have been salvaged from *Wisconsin's* bow. On the deck aft are some 5"/38 caliber gunhouses. (The last American fast battleship.)
NH 93589

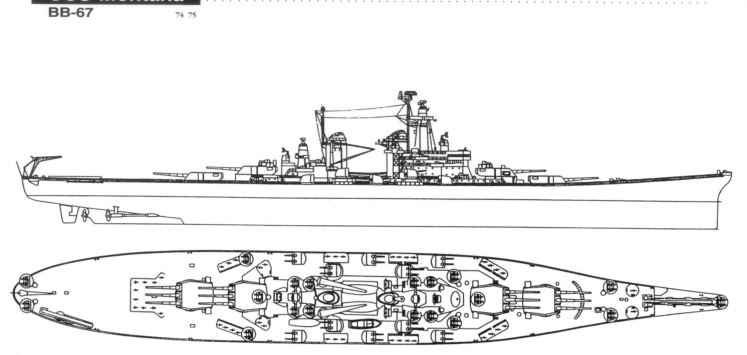

The *Montana* (BB 67) as designed (A. L. Raven).

Montana, line drawing by A. L. Raven shows how the *Montana* Class (BB-67 thru BB-71) would have looked if completed. Line drawing by A. L. Raven.

U.S. NAVAL INSTITUTE

1st Commanding Officer:
Authorized: July 19, 1940
Keel Laid: No
Launched: No
Commissioned: Cancelled July 21, 1943
Sponsor:
Displacement Standard Tons: 60,500
Displacement Full Load Tons: 70.965
Design Crew Complement: 115 officers, 2240 enlisted, Flagship 2789
Main Guns: 12-16" 50 caliber (41,600-yard range with armor-piercing rounds)
Secondary Guns: 20-5" / 54 caliber; 10 QUAD 40 millimeter AA; 56-20 millimeter AA
Construction Costs: $200 million (author's estimate)
Armor: Maximum thickness 18" at turret face plates
Length Overall: 890' waterline, 921' overall
Mean Draught: 36'4"
Extreme Beam: 115' waterline, 121'2" maximum
Torpedo Tubes: None
Catapults: 2, aft

Builder: Assigned to the Philadelphia Navy Yard
Original Engines Manufactured: Geared turbine
Original Boilers Manufactured: Babcock & Wilcox type
Original Fuel: Oil, 7500 tons (2,250,000 gallons)
Drive: Turbine, 4 screws
Sisters: *Montana* Class
Designed Speed: 28 knots
Designed Shaft Horsepower: 172,000
Design Comments: Designed to have been the ultimate in American battleship development
History Highlights:
· Name "*Montana*" assigned on Dec. 28, 1940
· Construction cancelled July 21, 1943 before the keel was laid
· With extreme beam as authorized, the *Montana* Class would not fit through the locks of the Panama Canal
Date Decommissioned:
Commendations: None
Final Disposition: Class suspended on May 20, 1942 and cancelled on July 21, 1943

1st Commanding Officer:

Authorized: July 19, 1940

Keel Laid: No

Launched: No

Commissioned: Cancelled July 21, 1943

Sponsor:

Displacement Standard Tons: 60,500

Displacement Full Load Tons: 70,965

Design Crew Complement: 115 officers, 2240 enlisted, Flagship 2789

Main Guns: 12-16" 50 caliber (41,600-yard range with armor-piercing rounds)

Secondary Guns: 20-5"/ 54 caliber; 10 QUAD 40 millimeter AA; 56-20 millimeter AA

Construction Costs: $200 million (author's estimate)

Armor: Maximum thickness 18" at turret face plates

Length Overall: 890' waterline, 921' overall

Mean Draught: 36'4"

Extreme Beam: 115' waterline, 121'2" maximum

Torpedo Tubes: None

Catapults: 2, aft

Builder: Assigned to the Philadelphia Navy Yard

Original Engines Manufactured: Geared turbine

Original Boilers Manufactured: Babcock & Wilcox type

Original Fuel: Oil, 7500 tons (2,250,000 gallons)

Drive: Turbine, 4 screws

Sisters: *Montana* Class

Designed Speed: 28 knots

Designed Shaft Horsepower: 172,000

Design Comments: Designed to have been the ultimate in American battleship development

History Highlights:
- Name "*Ohio*" assigned on Dec. 28, 1940
- Construction cancelled July 21, 1943 before the keel was laid
- With extreme beam as authorized, the *Montana* Class would not fit through the locks of the Panama Canal

Date Decommissioned:

Commendations: None

Final Disposition: Class suspended on May 20, 1942 and cancelled on July 21, 1943

Ohio, artist's conception of the *Montana* Class (BB-67 thru BB-71). These ships were cancelled on July 21, 1943. NH 61246

1st Commanding Officer:

Authorized: July 19, 1940

Keel Laid: No

Launched: No

Commissioned: Cancelled on July 21, 1943

Sponsor:

Displacement Standard Tons: 60,500

Displacement Full Load Tons: 70,965

Design Crew Complement: 115 officers, 2240 enlisted, Flagship 2789

Main Guns: 12-16" 50 caliber (41,600-yard range with armor-piercing rounds)

Secondary Guns: 20-5"/ 54 caliber; 10 QUAD 40 millimeter AA; 56-20 millimeter AA

Construction Costs: $200 million (author's estimate)

Armor: Maximum thickness 18" at turret face plates

Length Overall: 890' waterline, 921' overall

Mean Draught: 36'4"

Extreme Beam: 115' waterline, 121'2" maximum

Torpedo Tubes: None

Catapults: 2, aft

Builder: Assigned to the New York Navy Yard, Brooklyn, New York

Original Engines Manufactured: Geared turbine

Original Boilers Manufactured: Babcock & Wilcox type

Original Fuel: Oil, 7500 tons (2,250,000 gallons)

Drive: Turbine, 4 screws

Sisters: *Montana* Class

Designed Speed: 28 knots

Designed Shaft Horsepower: 172,000

Design Comments: Designed to have been the ultimate in American battleship development

History Highlights:

• Name "*Maine*" assigned on Dec. 28, 1940

• Construction cancelled July 21, 1943 before the keel was laid

• With extreme beam as authorized, the *Montana* Class would not fit through the locks of the Panama Canal

Date Decommissioned:

Commendations: None

Final Disposition: Class suspended on May 20, 1942 and cancelled on July 21, 1943

Maine, aft view of the ship model photographed at the New York Navy Yard, on Nov. 26, 1941. Ships intended for this design were: *Montana* (BB-67), *Ohio* (BB-68), *Maine* (BB-69), *New Hampshire* (BB-70), *Louisiana* (BB-71). NH 93914

1st Commanding Officer:

Authorized: July 19, 1940

Keel Laid: No

Launched: No

Commissioned: Cancelled on July 21, 1943

Sponsor:

Displacement Standard Tons: 60,500

Displacement Full Load Tons: 70,965

Design Crew Complement: 115 officers, 2240 enlisted, Flagship 2789

Main Guns: 12-16" 50 caliber (41,600-yard range with armor-piercing rounds)

Secondary Guns: 20-5" / 54 caliber; 10 QUAD 40 millimeter AA; 56-20 millimeter AA

Construction Costs: $200 million (author's estimate)

Armor: Maximum thickness 18" at turret face plates

Length Overall: 890' waterline, 921' overall

Mean Draught: 36'4"

Extreme Beam: 115' waterline, 121'2" maximum

Torpedo Tubes: None

Catapults: 2, aft

Builder: Assigned to the New York Navy Yard, Brooklyn, New York

Original Engines Manufactured: Geared turbine

Original Boilers Manufactured: Babcock & Wilcox type

Original Fuel: Oil, 7500 tons (2,250,000 gallons)

Drive: Turbine, 4 screws

Sisters: *Montana* Class

Designed Speed: 28 knots

Designed Shaft Horsepower: 172,000

Design Comments: Designed to have been the ultimate in American battleship development

History Highlights:

· Name "*New Hampshire*" assigned on Dec. 28, 1940

· Construction cancelled July 21, 1943 before the keel was laid

· With extreme beam as authorized, the *Montana* Class would not fit through the locks of the Panama Canal

Date Decommissioned:

Commendations: None

Final Disposition: Class suspended on May 20, 1942 and cancelled on July 21, 1943

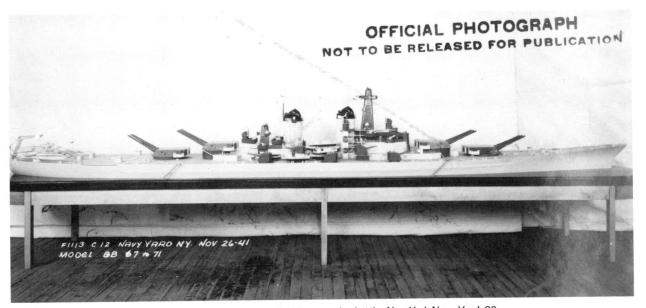

OFFICIAL PHOTOGRAPH
NOT TO BE RELEASED FOR PUBLICATION

New Hampshire, starboard broadside view of the ship model photographed at the New York Navy Yard, 26 november 1941. Ships planned for construction to this design were: *Montana* (BB-67), *Ohio* (BB-68), *Maine* (BB-69), *New Hampshire* (BB-70), *Louisiana* (BB-71). NH 93912

USS Louisiana
BB-71
74 75

1st Commanding Officer:

Authorized: July 19, 1940

Keel Laid: No

Launched: No

Commissioned: Cancelled on July 21, 1943

Sponsor:

Displacement Standard Tons: 60,500

Displacement Full Load Tons: 70,965

Design Crew Complement: 115 officers, 2240 enlisted, Flagship 2789

Main Guns: 12-16" 50 caliber (41,600-yard range with armor-piercing rounds)

Secondary Guns: 20-5"/ 54 caliber; 10 QUAD 40 millimeter AA; 56-20 millimeter AA

Construction Costs: $200 million (author's estimate)

Armor: Maximum thickness 18" at turret face plates

Length Overall: 890' waterline, 921' overall

Mean Draught: 36'4"

Extreme Beam: 115' waterline, 121'2" maximum

Torpedo Tubes: None

Catapults: 2, aft

Builder: Assigned to the Norfolk Navy Yard, Portsmouth, Virginia

Original Engines Manufactured: Geared turbine

Original Boilers Manufactured: Babcock & Wilcox type

Original Fuel: Oil, 7500 tons (2,250,000 gallons)

Drive: Turbine, 4 screws

Sisters: *Montana* Class

Designed Speed: 28 knots

Designed Shaft Horsepower: 172,000

Design Comments: Designed to have been the ultimate in American battleship development

History Highlights:

· Name "*Louisiana*" assigned on Dec. 28, 1940

· Construction cancelled July 21!, 1943 before the keel was laid

· With extreme beam as authorized, the *Montana* Class would not fit through the locks of the Panama Canal

Date Decommissioned:

Commendations: None

Final Disposition: Class suspended on May 20, 1942 and cancelled on July 21, 1943

Right: Louisiana, bow view of the ship model photographed at the New York Navy Yard, Nov. 26, 1941. Ships intended for this design were: *Montana* (BB-67), *Ohio* (BB-68), *Maine* (BB-69), *New Hampshire* (BB-70), *Louisiana* (BB-71). NH 93913

Below: Louisiana, the *Montana* Class would have had two sets of turrets as shown here on *Iowa* (BB-61) taken on Oct. 30, 1994 at the Philadelphia Navy Yard. These sets would have been two forward, turrets 1 and 2, and two aft, turrets 3 and 4. One can only imagine the massive firepower that could be brought to bear.

PERSONAL COLLECTION OF AUTHOR

102

Notes on Sources

Sources for the book were primarily taken from the *Dictionary of American Naval Fighting Ships*, the Franklin D. Roosevelt Library in Hyde Park, New York, the National Archives Cardigraphic, (microfilm rolls 5958-1,2,3 and 4 for the *South Dakota* class of 1919 and microfilm roll number 32106 for the *Montana* class), and the Still Pictures Branches in College Park, Maryland, the *U.S. Army-Navy Journal of Recognition*, September, 1943, Number 1, and excerpts with permission from the published individual battleship's history books.

Specific information on Fleet Anchorages and Naval Ordinances was taken and used with permission from *Jane's Fighting Ships of World War I* and *Jane's American Fighting Ships of the 20th Century*.

Technical information on the *Montana* (BB-67) class of 1940 was taken from *U.S. Battleships An Illustrated Design History*, by Norman Friedman and used with permission of the Naval Institute Press.

The line drawing of the *Montana* (BB-67) class of 1940 by A. L. Raven was taken from *U.S. Battleships An Illustrated Design History*, by Norman Friedman and used with permission of the author and the Naval Institute Press.

USS Arizona (BB-39) Ship's Data, A Photographic History by Norman Friedman, Arthur S. Lott, LCDR, USN (Ret), and Robert F. Sumrall, HTC, USS Arizona Memorial Museum Association, © 1978

USS California (BB-44) Golden State Battlewagon by Myron I. Smith, Jr. © 1983

USS Iowa (BB-61) Warships Data #3, by Robert F. Sumrall, © 1986

USS Maryland (BB-46) Free State Battlewagon by Myron J. Smith, Jr., © 1986

USS Massachusetts (BB-59) Ship's Data #8 by Norman Friedman, Arnold S. Lott, LDCR, USN (Ret), and Robert F. Sumrall, HTC, USNR, USS Massachusetts Memorial Committee, Inc., © 1985

USS Missouri (BB-63) Part 1: 1941–1984 Warships Data #2 by Robert F. Sumrall, © 1986, The Floating Drydock

USS North Carolina (BB-55), by Captain Ben W. Blee, USN (Ret), USS North Carolina Battleship Commission, © 1982

USS Pennsylvania (BB-38) Keystone Battlewagon by Myron J. Smith, Jr., © 1983

USS Tennessee (BB-43) Volunteer State Battlewagon by Myron J. Smith, Jr., © 1992

Battleship Texas (BB-35) by Hugh I. Power Jr., © 1993

USS West Virginia (BB-48) Mountaineer Battlewagon by Myron J. Smith, Jr., © 1982

U.S. Battleships, An Illustrated Design History by Norman Friedman Naval Institute Press, © 1985.

History of the U.S. Navy, by James M. Morris Brompton Books Corporation, © 1993

American Naval History by Jack Sweetman © 1992, United States Naval Institute

Battleship Country—The Battle Fleet at San Pedro—Long Beach, California 1919–1940 by Harvey M. Beigel, © 1983

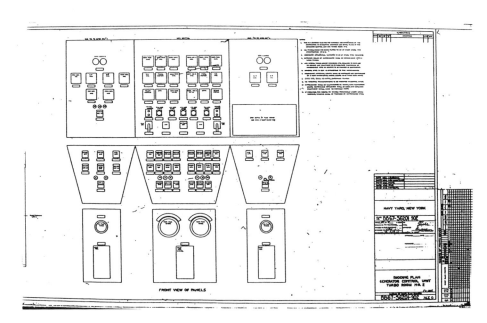

New Hampshire, line drawing taken from original ship's hull plan showing the bidding plan generator control unit, turbo room #2. Identified to New York Navy Yard possibly for *New Hampshire* (BB-70) or M*aine* (BB-69). Both assigned to New York Navy Yard.

NATIONAL ARCHIVES
MICROFILM ROLL 32106

SUGGESTED FURTHER READING

Individual battleships data books

USS Alabama (BB-60) Ship's Data Book, USS Alabama Gift Shop, 256 Summit Street South, Fairhope, AL 36532

USS Arizona (BB-39) Ship's Data, A Photographic History, by Norman Friedman, Arthur S. Lott, LCDR, USN (Ret), and Robert F. Sumrall, HTC, USNR, Arizona Memorial Museum Association, © 1978 No. 1 Arizona Memorial Pl. Honolulu, HI 96818

USS California (BB-44) Golden State Battlewagon by Myron I. Smith, Jr. © 1983 Pictorial Histories Publishing Co., 713 South 3rd, West Missoula, MT 59801

USS Iowa (BB-61) Warships Data #3 by Robert F. Sumrall, © 1986 Pictorial Histories Publishing Co., 713 South 3rd West, Missoula, MT 59801

USS Maryland (BB-46) Free State Battlewagon by Myron J. Smith, Jr., © 1986 Pictorial Histories Publishing Co., 13 South 3rd West, Missoula, MT 59801

USS Massachusetts (BB-59) Ships Data #8, by Norman Friedman, Arnold S. Lott, LDCR, USN (Ret), and Robert F. Sumrall, HTC, USNR, *USS Massachusetts* Memorial Committee, Inc., © 1985 Battleship Cove, Fall River, MA 02721

USS Missouri (BB-63) Part 1: 1941-1984 Warships Data #2 by Robert F. Sumrall, © 1986, The Floating Drydock, Pictorial Histories Publishing Co., 713 South 3rd West, Missoula MT 59801

USS North Carolina (BB-55) by Captain Ben W. Blee, USN (Ret), *USS North Carolina* Battleship Commission, © 1982 P.O. Box 480, Wilmington, NC 28402

USS Pennsylvania (BB-38) Keystone Battlewagon by Myron J. Smith, Jr., © 1983 Pictorial Histories Publishing Co., 713 South 3rd West, Missoula, MT 59801

USS Tennessee (BB-43) Volunteer State Battlewagon by Myron J. Smith, Jr., © 1992 Pictorial Histories Publishing Co., 713 South 3rd West, Missoula, MT 59801

Battleship Texas (BB-35) by Hugh I. Power Jr., © 1993 Texas A&M University Press, College Station, TX 77843

USS West Virginia (BB-48) Mountaineer Battlewagon by Myron J. Smith, Jr., © 1982 Pictorial Histories Publishing Co., 713 South 3rd West, Missoula MT 59801

Books on all/class of Battleship

Steel Ships and Iron Men by Bruce Roberts and Ray Jones, © 1991 Globe Pequot Press 138 West Main Street Chester, CT 06412

Dictionary of American Naval Fighting Ships (8 Volume Set) Superintendent of Documents U.S. Government Printing Office Washington, DC 20402

U.S. Battleships, An Illustrated Design History by Norman Friedman © 1985, United States Naval Institute Naval Institute PressAnnapolis, MD 21402

Conway's All the World's Battleships Edited by Ian Sturton © 1987, United States Naval Institute Naval Institute Press Annapolis, MD 21402

The Iowa Class Battleships by Malcolm Muir, Jr., © 1987 Dorset Press New York, NY

U.S. Battleships in Action, Part 1 & Part 2, by Robert C. Stern Squadron/Signal Publications, Inc.© 1980 & © 1984 Respectively Carrollton, TX 75011-5010

U.S. Naval Developments, by Jan S. Breemer, © 1983 The Nautical and Aviation Publishing Company of AmericaBaltimore, MD 21201

Naval Engineering and American Sea Power, Edited by Rear Admiral R.W. King, USN (Ret) © 1989, The American Society of Naval Engineers, The Nautical and Aviation Publishing Company of America Baltimore, MD 21201

This People's Navy, The Making of American Sea Power by Kenneth J. Hagan The Free Press, © 1991 A Division of Macmillan, Inc. New York, NY 10022

History of the U.S. Navy by James M. Morris Brompton Books Corporation, © 1984 & © 1993 Greenwich, CT 06830

Sacred Vessels, The Cult of the Battleship and the Rise of the U.S. Navy, by Robert L. O'Connell, Oxford University Press

American Naval History, by Jack Sweetman © 1992, United States Naval Institute, Naval Institute Press, Annapolis, MD 21402-5035

Battleship Country—The Battle Fleet at San Pedro— Long Beach, California 1919–1940 by Harvey M. Beigel, © 1983 Pictorial Histories Publishing Co., 713 South 3rd West, Missoula MT 59801

Jane's Fighting Ships of World War I © Studio Editions, Limited 50 Eastcastle Road London, W1N 7AP, United Kingdom, Current Edition, © 1990 by Military Press, New York NY 10003

Jane's American Fighting Ships of the 20th Century © Studio Editions, Limited 50 Eastcastle Road London, W1N 7AP, United Kingdom, Current Edition © 1991 by Mallard Press New York NY 10103

USS New Jersey—The Navy's Big Guns (From Mothballs to Vietnam), by Neil Leifer, © 1988, & Robert F. Dorr, Motorbrooks International Osceola, WI 54020

Desert Storm, Sea War, by Arnold Meisner, © 1991 Motorbrooks International Publishers & Wholesalers, P.O. Box 2, 729 Prospect Avenue, Osceola WI 54020

FOOTNOTES

....

1 James M. Morris, *History of the U.S. Navy*, Brompton Books Corporation, 1993; pp. 51–52.

2. James M. Morris, *History of the U.S. Navy*, Brompton Books Corporation, 1993; p. 64.

3. James M. Morris, *History of the U.S. Navy*, Brompton Books Corporation, 1993; p. 65.

4. Norman Friedman, *U.S. Battleships*, An Illustrated Design History, Naval Institute Press, 1985; pp. 149–153.

5. Jack Sweetman, *American Naval History*, United States Naval Institute, 1992; pp. 103–109.

6. James M. Morris, *History of the U.S. Navy*, Brompton Books Corporation, 1993; p. 73.

7. Norman Friedman, *U.S. Battleships*, An Illustrated Design History, Naval Institute Press, 1985; pp. 149–153.

8. Norman Friedman, *U.S. Battleships*, An Illustrated Design History, Naval Institute Press, 1985; p. 171.

9. Harvey M. Beigel, *Battleship Country, The Battle Fleet at San Pedro—Long Beach, California 1919–1940, 1983*; p. 1.

10. James M. Morris, *History of the U.S. Navy*, Brompton Books Corporation, 1993; p. 95.

11. Harvey M. Beigel, *Battleship Country, The Battle Fleet at San Pedro—Long Beach, California 1919–1940, 1983*; p. 49.

12. Harvey M. Beigel, *Battleship Country, The Battle Fleet at San Pedro—Long Beach, California 1919–1940, 1983*; p. 63.

13. Norman Friedman, Arthur S. Lott, LCDR, USN (Ret), and Robert F. Sumrall, HTC, USNR, *USS Arizona (BB-39) Ship's Data, A Photographic History*, Arizona Memorial Museum Association, 1978; pp. 45, 46.

14. Norman Friedman, Arthur S. Lott, LCDR, USN (Ret), and Robert F. Sumrall, HTC, USNR, *USS Massachusetts (BB-59)*, Ships Data #8, USS Massachusetts Memorial Committee, Inc., 1985; p. 18.

15. Hugh I. Power, Jr., *Battleship Texas, 1993*; p. 23.

16. Myron J. Smith, *USS Maryland (BB-46)*, Free State Battlewagon, 1986; p. 27.

17. Captain Ben W. Blee, USN (Ret), *USS North Carolina (BB-55)*, USS North Carolina Battleship Commission, 1982; pp. 46–50.

18. Hugh I. Power, Jr., *Battleship Texas, 1993*; p. 25.

19. Myron J. Smith, Jr., *USS Tennessee (BB-43)*, Volunteer State Battlewagon, 1992; p. 36.

20. Captain Ben W. Blee, USN (Ret), *USS North Carolina (BB-55)*, USS North Carolina Battleship Commission, 1982; p. 96.

21. Norman Friedman, Arthur S. Lott, LCDR, USN (Ret), and Robert F. Sumrall, HTC, USNR, *USS Massachusetts (BB-59)*, Ships Data #8, USS Massachusettes Memorial Committee, Inc., 1985; p. 26.

22. Myron J. Smith, Jr., *USS Pennsylvania (BB-38)*, Keystone Battlewagon, 1983, p. 30.

23. Myron J. Smith, Jr., *USS Tennessee (BB-43)*, Volunteer State Battlewagon, 1992; p. 37.

24. Hugh I. Power, Jr., *Battleship Texas, 1993*; p. 24.

25. Hugh I. Power, Jr., *Battleship Texas, 1993*; pp. 29, 30.

26. Hugh I. Power, Jr., *Battleship Texas, 1993*; p. 31.

27. Captain Ben W. Blee, USN (Ret), *USS North Carolina (BB-55)*, USS North Carolina Battleship Commission, 1982; p. 65.

28. Myron J. Smith, Jr., *USS Tennessee (BB-43)*, Volunteer State Battlewagon, 1992; pp. 38, 39.

29. Robert F. Sumrall, *USS Iowa (BB-61)*, Warships Data #3, 1986; p. 41.

30. Captain Ben W. Blee, USN (Ret), *USS North Carolina (BB-55)*, USS North Carolina Battleship Commission, 1982; pp. 70, 71.

31. Myron J. Smith, Jr., *USS Tennessee (BB-43)*, Volunteer State Battlewagon, 1992; p. 42.

32. Myron J. Smith, Jr., *USS Tennessee (BB-43)*, Volunteer State Battlewagon, 1992; p. 36.

33. Myron J. Smith, Jr., *USS Tennessee (BB-43)*, Volunteer State Battlewagon, 1992; p. 43.

34. Robert F. Sumrall, *USS Iowa (BB-61)*, Warships Data #3, 1986, p. 42.

35. Myron J. Smith, Jr., *USS Tennessee (BB-43)*, Volunteer State Battlewagon, 1992; p. 43.

36. Myron J. Smith, Jr., *USS Maryland (BB-46)*, Free State Battlewagon, 1986; p. 39.

37. Myron J. Smith, Jr., *USS West Virginia (BB-48)*, Mountaineer Battlewagon, 1982; p. 35.

38. Myron J. Smith, Jr., *USS California (BB-44)*, Golden State Battlewagon, 1983; p. 37.

39. Myron J. Smith, Jr., *USS Tennessee (BB-43)*, Volunteer State Battlewagon, 1992; p. 44.

40. Myron J. Smith, Jr., *USS West Virginia (BB-48)*, Mountaineer Battlewagon, 1982; p. 45.

41. Myron J. Smith, Jr., *USS Maryland (BB-46)*, Free State Battlewagon, 1986; p. 40.

42. Robert F. Sumrall, *USS Missouri (BB-63)*, Part 1: 1941-1984 Warships Data #2, The Floating Drydock, 1986; p. 24.

43. Myron J. Smith, Jr., *USS Tennessee (BB-43)*, Volunteer State Battlewagon, 1992; p. 46.

44. Norman Friedman, Arthur S. Lott, LCDR, USN (Ret), and Robert F. Sumrall, HTC, USNR, *USS Massachusetts (BB-59)*, Ships Data #8, USS Massachusettes Memorial Committee, Inc., 1985; p. 29.

45. Myron J. Smith, Jr., *USS Pennsylvania (BB-38)*, Keystone Battlewagon, 1983; p. 34.

46. Norman Friedman, Arthur S. Lott, LCDR, USN (Ret), and Robert F. Sumrall, HTC, USNR, *USS Arizona (BB-39) Ship's Data, A Photographic History*, Arizona Memorial Museum Association, 1978; p. 48.

47. Captain Ben W. Blee, USN (Ret), *USS North Carolina (BB-55)*, USS North Carolina Battleship Commission, 1982; p. 92.

48. James M. Morris, *History of the U.S. Navy*, Brompton Books Corporation, 1993; p. 216.

49. Robert F. Sumrall, *USS Iowa (BB-61)*, Warships Data #3, 1986; p. 54.

50. Robert F. Sumrall, *USS Iowa (BB-61)*, Warships Data #3, 1986; p. 50.

51. James M. Morris, *History of the U.S. Navy*, Brompton Books Corporation, 1993; pp. 238–241.

52. Harvey M. Beigel, *Battleship Country, The Battle Fleet at San Pedro—Long Beach, California 1919–1940, 1983*; p. 1.

53. Norman Friedman, *U.S. Battleships*, An Illustrated Design History, Naval Institute Press, 1985; p. 166.

54. *Jane's Fighting Ships of World War I*, Studio Editions, Limited, Princess House, United Kingdom, 1990; p. 128.

55. *Jane's American Fighting Ships of the 20th Century*, Studio Editions, Limited, Princess House, United Kingdom, 1990; p. 22.

56. Robert F. Sumrall, *USS Iowa (BB-61)*, Warships Data #3, 1986; pp. 52, 53.

57. Captain Ben W. Blee, USN (Ret), *USS North Carolina (BB-55)*, USS North Carolina Battleship Commission, 1982; p. 95.

58. Norman Friedman, Arthur S. Lott, LCDR, USN (Ret), and Robert F. Sumrall, HTC, USNR, *USS Arizona (BB-39) Ship's Data, A Photographic History*, Arizona Memorial Museum Association, 1978; p. 51.

59. Robert F. Sumrall, *USS Iowa (BB-61)*, Warships Data #3, 1986; pp. 52, 53.

60. Norman Friedman, Arthur S. Lott, LCDR, USN (Ret), and Robert F. Sumrall, HTC, USNR, *USS Massachusetts (BB-59)*, Ships Data #8, USS Massachusettes Memorial Committee, Inc., 1985; p. 32.

61. Norman Friedman, Arthur S. Lott, LCDR, USN (Ret), and Robert F. Sumrall, HTC, USNR, *USS Arizona (BB–39) Ship's Data, A Photographic History*, Arizona Memorial Museum Association, 1978; p. 51.

62. Hugh I. Power, Jr., *Battleship Texas, 1993*; pp. 131, 134.

63. Myron J. Smith, Jr., *USS Pennsylvania (BB-38)*, Keystone Battlewagon, 1983; p. 44.

64. Norman Friedman, Arthur S. Lott, LCDR, USN (Ret), and Robert F. Sumrall, HTC, USNR, *USS Arizona (BB-39) Ship's Data, A Photographic History*, Arizona Memorial Museum Association 1978; pp. 50, 51.

65. Myron J. Smith, Jr., *USS Tennessee (BB-43)*, Volunteer State Battlewagon, 1992; p. 56.

66. Myron I. Smith, Jr., *USS California (BB-44)*, Golden State Battlewagon, 1983; p. 44.

67. Myron J. Smith, Jr., *USS Maryland (BB-46)*, Free State Battlewagon, 1986; p. 48.

68. Myron J. Smith, Jr., *USS West Virginia (BB-48)*, Mountaineer Battlewagon, 1982; p. 48.

69. NARA (Information on Waterline Model of BB-52 & Ships profiles).

70. Norman Friedman, *U.S. Battleships*, An Illustrated Design History, Naval Institute Press, 1985; p. 446.

71. Captain Ben W. Blee, USN (Ret), *USS North Carolina (BB-55)*, USS North Carolina Battleship Commission, 1982; pp. 94, 95.

72. Norman Friedman, Arthur S. Lott, LCDR, USN (Ret), and Robert F. Sumrall, HTC, USNR, *USS Massachusetts (BB-59)*, Ships Data #8, USS Massachusettes Memorial Committee, Inc., 1985; pp. 31,32.

73. Robert F. Sumrall, *USS Iowa (BB-61)*, Warships Data #3, 1986; pp. 52, 53.

74. Norman Friedman, *U.S. Battleships*, An Illustrated Design History, Naval Institute Press, 1985; p. 450.

75. A. L.Raven,(line drawing), Norman Friedman, *U.S. Battleships*, An Illustrated Design History, Naval Institute Press, 1985; p. 340.

ABOUT THE AUTHOR

. . . .

MAX HAS BEEN A HISTORY ENTHUSIAST for many years, and developed the idea of his book as he began reading and acquiring the information and history of the American battleships. He is the Engineering Manager at Lehigh Fluid Power in Lambertville, NJ, and resides with his wife Elizabeth in Buckingham, PA.

Background in photo is *USS Olympia,* a memorial in Philadelphia, Pa. Photo taken Oct. 30, 1994. *Olympia* was Admiral Dewey's Flagship at the Battle of Manila Bay in the Philippines during the Spanish-American War. May 1, 1898